From Amish to Apostolic

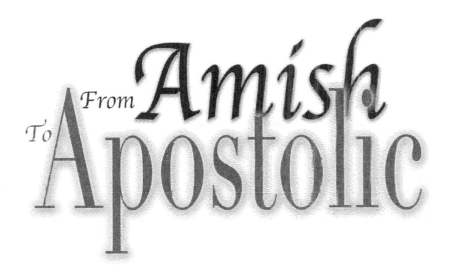

From Amish To Apostolic

Audrey Feigl

CLASSIC
PUBLISHING

Dover, Delaware

Unless otherwise indicated, all Scripture quotations are taken from the King James Version of the Bible.

From Amish To Apostolic
ISBN 978-0-9747414-7-5
Copyright 2008 by Audrey Feigl

Audrey Feigl
29 Smith Road
Gardners, PA 17324

Published by
Classic Publishing
Dover, Delaware
www.myclassicpublishing.com

Cover Design:
Angela Carrington
Inspire Media, LLC

Contents

Acknowledgements

Thanks to my sister and brother-in-law, Geraldine and Thomas White for their encouragement in this project, and to the people at my work site also, for cheering me on. A special word of thanks and praise goes to Jesus Christ, our Lord, for putting us in touch with people willing to do the manuscript form in its final stage. Without Greg Frankford, Microsoft Word would have been tossed out the window. Thanks, Brother Greg, for rescuing me. My heartfelt appreciation will always be with Brother David King and his precious wife, Barbara, for trusting my judgment in recording their brief but engaging account of transition from Amish to Apostolic. God bless all of you. And, how could I ever miss thanking my buddy, Linda Ackerman, who fortifies my weak points and really believes in me.

Preface

From Amish to Apostolic was penned through personal interviews and written correspondence. This book was not written in story form but rather follows the personal feelings and recalls specific times of change in David and Barbara's lives. The ordinary life of Old Order Amish tradition is disrupted by changes of varying degrees. David especially becomes determined to find his answers to spiritual matters outside the familiar boundaries. Barbara, on the other hand, tries to continue in a more stable fashion to remain within the Amish faith. In due time, however, they must decide the outcome of their search for truth. The Kings pass through a soul searching period before making a final break. Their testimonies conclude the book along with a word from John Brown and his wife, Charlene, the people most involved in teaching them the Word of God.

Foreword

Pentecost in the Amish Community

Three hundred years ago, the Plain People began to migrate to North America. They left their homes and farms in Europe forever. Today, Amish are found in over 250 settlements across 33 states. There are four main groups of Amish and many sub-groups of Mennonites. In many settlements there has been a shift from farming to laborers and entrepreneurs. This transformation has offered an incredible opportunity to present the Apostolic truth to them. The occupational change has begun to reshape the identity and texture of the Amish and Mennonite life.

The Amish and Mennonite people have a strong belief in the divinity of Christ. Across North America, Apostolics are discovering that these devout people can be led into the full truth. They live clean lives and have strong families. The Holy Bible is seen as a sacred trust; they interpret it literally and directly.

Since they practice excommunication for serious offenses, such as re-baptism, it is important to be aware of their culture. If an Amish person is re-baptized, the Amish elders think they have renounced their former baptism and they excommunicate them. As a result, the individual must cope with the emotions of being betrayed, humiliated and alienated. Their closest

Foreword

friends and family "shun" them. They need special attention and friendship after they are baptized in Jesus' name and filled with the Holy Spirit.

We are hearing of a steady flow of people leaving the Amish community because they are spiritually hungry. As they begin to reach out, it important that we are present to lead them into the truth. In Lancaster County, Pennsylvania, approximately 40 families left the Amish because of their spiritual hunger. David and Barbara King, and their eight children, responded to weekly Bible studies in Virginia. They are now actively engaged in helping other Amish find the truth. David said, "After my baptism, I was rejected and persecuted by my people because of what I did." The elders of the Amish church did not like the news that he had been re-baptized and demanded that he renounce it. He "did not back down" and the elders excommunicated them. The days following were difficult but God rewarded the sacrifice by healing Barbara's eyes. She has not needed glasses since.

John Wayne and RoseAnna Mullett made the journey from Amish to Apostolic. John, age 29, and RoseAnna, age 28 were given a better understanding of the Word by Elmer and Pam Miller. Rose said, "My shoulder was miraculously healed the day that I was baptized."

Foreword

Ernie and Mary Jess made a trip to Indiana from Illinois for Christmas. They stopped in to see John and RoseAnna. After searching the Word and studying what they had been told, they decided to be baptized in Jesus' name by immersion. Mary fasted the 8 days leading up to baptism. Ernie's family found out about the plans before the baptism and came to their home. Many tears were shed. The pain of misunderstanding was difficult. Ernie's employer stopped in on Saturday and told him he would be fired and that he should not come back to work on Monday, if he proceeded with baptism. Their landlord gave 30 days notice to move out of their home if they were baptized. The persecution was immediate and strong.

On the following Sunday, they were baptized in the name of Jesus. Mary received the Holy Ghost while she was still in the tank. She said, "I had never felt anything like it before. The peace and joy can't be described. It was a revelation." Ernie received the Holy Ghost a couple months later. A former Mennonite, Richard Gingrich, was baptized the same day.

Jonathan Miller was walking out to the barn in Kentucky when he thought he heard someone speak to him. He turned around to look but saw no one. He recalled, "Walking three steps farther, I found myself frozen. I couldn't move, nor could I speak." Thinking "this must be my time", he said, "here I am

Foreword

Lord, I'm all yours." Suddenly the form of a person appeared in front of him. Jonathan said, "The form was glowing so bright that I had to squint my eyes to see." The form had one hand raised and spoke to him: "Be obedient. Preach the Word of God and teach the plan of salvation!" That experience was quite a departure from the prayer book used to communicate with God.

Abram and Alma Toews journeyed from the Mennonite church into the truth. As a door-to-door salesman, Abram often took his briefcase and Bible and hid in the woods to read, pray and weep for answers. After months of teaching by Brother J. P. Vogt, God gave them the revelation of the Godhead and baptism in Jesus name. They were baptized in a gravel pit filled with water.

Lillian King grew up in an Old Order Amish home in Lancaster County, Pennsylvania. At seventeen, she decided to join the New Order Amish Church. Her spiritual hunger led her to various Mennonite churches but to no avail. At age 26, she found a Pentecostal church in the newspaper. When she walked in she said, "I felt something I had never felt before. I cried when they sang. When I heard Acts 2:38 for the first time, I knew this was what I had been looking for."

Foreword

This past Sunday night, Rachael was brought to our church in North East, Maryland, by David & Barbara King and Elmer & Pam Miller. They had heard of her intense hunger for spiritual nourishment. Brother Trout privately spoke to the music director and asked her to use well-known, traditional hymns on Sunday evening. He did not want her first Apostolic service to be such a jolt. The service had already begun when they walked in. I ushered them to the front pew and sat with Rachael and her two children. Before I could get settled into the pew, she was on her feet, waving her hands and singing the songs. Her hunger had her on her feet, worshipping intensely most of the service. When the altar was opened, we walked to the front and within minutes, she was speaking with tongues. We baptized her immediately. That is, as soon as we could settle her down enough to change into the robe. After baptism, she spent the next two hours dancing around the church with the saints.

The Amish are hard working, humble and God-fearing people. However, to leave the Amish church is to be cut off from family and friends in the community. Shunning is a high price and great sacrifice. Let's not overlook their qualities and values as we share the revelation that they have not yet received.

Janet Trout
Amish-Mennonite Evangelism Ministry Director
United Pentecostal Church International

Introduction

There are times in history when God asserts His sovereign will. This was so during the era of the prophets, the apostles of Jesus Christ and throughout mankind's history. He moves in His own right upon the hungry hearts of men and women, those He created for His own glory. He uses individual contacts to further the cause of His glorious kingdom, the kingdom where righteousness dwells in the souls of the individuals seeking Him. His sovereignty allows the choice of time and place and consequently the ones to whom His revelation will come. Such was the choice at Azusa Street at the turn of the twentieth century and such has it been in the world today. In the year 2000, another turn of the century, God designed a personal intervention with David and Barbara King. It was not without personal struggles or because the road ahead looked easy that this couple chose to follow God into that marvelous light called the gospel of Jesus Christ.

Raised in the Old Order Amish, the Kings persevered to overcome great obstacles in order to call Jesus their great God and Savior. This book attempts to lead the reader into that fascinating realm of the tradition of separation from all modern conveniences, indeed, from all Englishers as non-Amish citizens are labeled. Go through the everyday life with the Amish as it is and has been for centuries. Feel the heartbeat of David and Barbara when God lays His powerful but loving hand on them to lead them from the traditions of men to the full truth of God's Word. They have traveled the length of centuries to embrace the doctrine of the twelve apostles Jesus called to establish His church on earth. From Amish to Apostolic is written with a prayer that a blessing of knowledge and better understanding of the operation of God's Spirit will be imparted to those who will trust Him, especially those in the Amish-Mennonite movement. If just one more soul finds the peace that passes all understanding, then this undertaking will not have been in vain.

Chapter One
Along the Rhine

$\mathcal{T}$he man was well known along the Rhine in many European cities. He had traveled a long road from his home to the New World of America and back. Now in the late 1600's, he had a definite purpose for traveling the river through Europe. He had faced religious persecution and was determined to establish a refuge for others enduring the same.

His audiences were the various occupants along the Rhine where activity bustled daily. His Religious Society of Friends, (Quakers), held out against terrible odds of ever having religious freedom in Europe. The state church had dominated since the fourth century when Constantine, Emperor of Rome, supposedly became a Christian. Any who opposed the religious order of the day suffered many hardships, even to martyrdom. Thus it was that William Penn determined to make his refuge

1

known. To the struggling masses of Europe, life where freedom of worship existed was an inviting topic. Penn had already begun his colony in the New World known as Pennsylvania; now the persecuted could come to this haven. Long before the sixteenth century, house groups began to come together to worship and to discuss their feelings on new technology and Christendom. Even before Martin Luther arrived on the scene, from whence we mark the Great Reformation, simple men and women were breaking away from the Catholic Church. Great struggles followed every group that persisted in leaving the state church. At the same time Luther was advocating church reform, the same move was occurring in Switzerland.

A former Dutch priest, Menno Simons, was converted to a group called the Anabaptists. The word comes from a Latin term, "anabaptismus," or "baptized again." They were rebaptized outside the state church and also rebelled against the Reformists. They claimed the church and state should be separated; also the Reformed Church had continued performing mass and infant baptism, which was condemned by the Anabaptists. The year was 1536 when Simons was converted and shortly became the most influential leader of the group. The decision was made to name his following the Mennonites. The Old Order Mennonites opposed war, violence, and serving in the military.

The Anabaptists stood their ground which brought swift retribution from both sides of the religious movements. The state church and the reformers brought not only reprimands, but severe persecution upon them. Those in rebellion thought the Reformed Church had not gone far enough in opposing the Catholic Church. Thousands of Anabaptists suffered death and torture from 1527 to 1727. Is it any wonder that the ones who could escape to the Americas took the chance? The trip was long and hard but at least there was hope. It was William Penn who held that hope out to them as a beacon in the darkest night.

While lords and clerics thrived well in life, the common man was, in essence, suffering from starvation.

Chapter Two
German Peasant's War

Authors who researched the war known as the German Peasant's War place the advent of the Anabaptist movement parallel with or even before that time. The great uprising began in April of 1525, but was suppressed shortly thereafter. The peasants lost their cause but continued the rebellion crisscrossing the time frame with subsequent skirmishes. Their cause cannot be separated from societal factors of the era. Theology was deeply involved in everyday life. The Anabaptists were, in fact, looking into scripture to validate the authority of their overseers. The feudal system of landlords, who were in complete control of the lives of the serfs, was hotly questioned. The most distinguishing factor was not the secular issue, but rather how the clerics dominated the group as a whole. While lords and clerics thrived well in life, the common man was, in essence, suffering from starvation.

The printing press was used to speed along the fiery indignation of Otto Brunfels, a pastor who published a tract in 1524 in Strasbourg, Germany. He condemned the collecting of tithes from the poor that found a resting place in bulging pockets of religious chapters and monasteries. Part of his rebuke was eventually called a manifesto against, as he wrote, "Those idle, rich, fat beggars, who grasp lands and meadows, which skin and steal from the whole world." This stinging revilement of the Catholic Church and land owners subject to the clergy was first printed in Latin and later reprinted to benefit the Reformists. This, no doubt, satiated the palate of many rebellious individuals who were repulsing the ideology of Catholicism. It did little good for the Anabaptist who refused to conform to the new mode of thinking presented by the Reformers.

The Anabaptists found themselves caught between persecutions from both groups. Brunfels continued his laceration of them all in his pamphlet. "Those," wrote he, "who compel the poor to pay tithes with their godless, devilish ban, and have no better justification for this than to sing mass seven times daily are viler betrayers of Christ than Judas, yes, than the godless priests of Baal." There were three levels of the feudal system, ruled by a hierarchy of clerics. The local king (lord) owned the land that was held by vassals. These in turn supplied the means of military duty and other services. The bottom man, the serf, in turn worked the land. Restless individuals who could at least read and interpret the literature at hand became openly hostile to the feudal system. The Anabaptists were not farmers originally but were made up of varying craftsmen who dwelt in the cities. It was through preaching and pamphlets of controversy that the Anabaptists were stirred to resist the established state-church. They did, however, seek scriptural guidance for all their actions. It is difficult to separate the German Peasant's War from the religious unrest that finally thrust Anabaptists from city life to the countryside. Their survival then rested upon skills and knowledge that carried them wave by wave to the New World.

During the 1600's alone, about 4,000 people were jailed,
women were buried alive, some others beheaded,
and many sold as galley slaves who were
forced to propel ships until they died.

Chapter Three
The Order of Life

The Anabaptist movement in general believes in an unwritten rule called the Ordnung; that is, the order of life, the whole way of life. There is no argument about clothing, work habits, church or family duties. While the man is distinctly head of the family, both father and mother are responsible for the training of children in religion and their place in the home. If a family is fortunate enough to have both genders of children, manpower for both field and home is supplied. The Anabaptists welcome large families and usually have several children. In this religious order, no provision is made for divorce, except for the case of adultery.

When one speaks of Anabaptist tradition, the tendency is to focus on the Amish. They are more separated in lifestyle and dress than others but are not distinguished entirely from Old

Order Mennonites, Hutterites, Beachy Amish, and others. They all collectively suffered tremendously in Europe. Eventually their non-violence was a resolve that brought thousands to death's door. During the 1600's alone, about 4,000 people were jailed, women were buried alive, some others beheaded, and many sold as galley slaves who were forced to propel ships until they died. They endured all of this because it was the Ordnung, the way of peace, the non-resistant life against evil they felt necessary to have in representation of the true church of Jesus Christ in their day. This was part of the reasoning for adults alone to be baptized into the church.

A great deal of self-examination must take place before joining the ranks, thus leaving infants and children insufficient to understand the ritual. There could be no turning back once baptism took place. To regress into a worldly lifestyle brought correction from the elders, and open repentance before the church. If for any reason the offender failed his part, he would be set out of the church. Excommunication was the lot for all who left the Anabaptist movement along with shunning. Menno Simons, the greatest influence upon the Anabaptist of Europe, held a strict line of authority in this. Again, the unwritten law of obedience prevailed. To resist this law brought harsh results to the one being judged.

Chapter Four
New Order Out of the Old

*I*n the late 1600's, a young Swiss church elder, Jakob Ammann, of the Mennonite movement, thought existing church discipline too lax. Although Menno Simons advocated the banning of members who did not live up to expectations, Ammann wanted a stricter order. Not much information remains about Ammann but we know his actions caused a splintering from the Mennonite group. They held to the same principles as the Mennonites, such as no infant baptisms, which was an abomination to them; non-violence was also preached and this Anabaptist group held to a peaceful way of life. In 1693, the movement took his name and is still called Old Order Amish. His reform took place 168 years after the initial beginning of the Anabaptists movement.

The Amish, as other Anabaptist groups, did not really desire to leave their homeland but persecution had driven them from land to land across Europe. They learned to manage and transform unproductive land into fertile, cultivated soil. During the 1600's, they excelled in Switzerland, Germany, and Alsace (France) by rotating crops and growing varieties of clover to restore the soil. They are the first known to feed cattle indoors,use animal fertilizer and learned to irrigate crops. All of this led to the ability to survive.

The Biblical account in Genesis and parables in the New Testament were the foundation of Anabaptists belief for farming. The Amish particularly believe farming is their God given command to be good stewards of the earth. Farmers work together as families and the survival issue caused these people to band together as communities. William Penn and the Quakers had long envisioned this type of movement. They, the Amish, could establish such colonies in the New World.

Chapter Five
Penn's Influence Works

The fever grew rapidly throughout the Anabaptist ranks until finally on October 2, 1727, several names of Amish families were found among those leaving Rotterdam on the ship, Adventure. A crossing could last up to eighty days and yet they boarded ship with some glimmer of hope. Philadelphia was their destination. Life aboard ship was anything but pleasant for the poor. They made their beds top deck in unthinkable conditions. Not enough clean water and lack of food brought sickness and death to the weakest, especially the children. At times, it seemed even the strongest became surly and discontented. Another discouraging factor was the thieves who often wreaked havoc among the helpless peasants.

Ten years later, in 1737, twenty-one Amish families boarded the Charming Nancy to settle in the counties of Berks,

Lancaster, and Chester, Pennsylvania. Life was not charmed even in a free land. Stories related to those early years bring a note of true compassion to the reader. For instance, if a traveler failed to have enough money for his fare, he was sold as an indentured servant. It never mattered that his goods were confiscated by English customs in the colony, or that his money was stolen, he was sold.

Elias B. Riehl told the story of his grandfather, Lewis Riehl, 1746-1806. Lewis was stolen away in Europe at eight years of age and brought to America. He was sold as a servant. When his time was completed, an Amish minister, Christian Zook and his family, took him into their care. Riehl converted to the faith and married Veronica Fisher. And so the Anabaptists came with heartaches, trials, and deprivation, searching for a land to call home.

Chapter Six
Here to Stay

The lessons learned in Europe served the Amish well. Being self-sufficient in all the necessities of everyday life would now support the group who had been harassed and deprived of a decent livelihood. In Sainte-Marie-Aux-Mines (France), they had become skilled in clearing land for agriculture. Their new home afforded ample opportunity to prove the worth of past lessons. Mostly forested land was available to newcomers; however, much toil, long hours, and almost impossible situations would gradually pay good dividends. The Amish now could actually own their farms. As time passed, the westward trek caught the fancy of some settlers to travel farther west. The Amish reached favorable spots in Ohio and communities rose up there. More tests awaited the pilgrims because the red man was now being pushed from his own territory. The new trials did not deter them in their quest for more land. Prevail they must if all were to have enough farm land for future generations.

Those were the days of great evangelism and soul searching endeavors. Just prior to the Revolutionary War, a stir was in the land again for greater purity in the faith. The Old Order people felt there was an indifference to spiritual matters. In 1903, C. I. B. Brane wrote of an Amishman, Abraham Drasksel (1753) a minister in Lebanon County, Pennsylvania, who came under the influence of Protestant revivalists. He was quickly warned of making too much of the doctrine of regeneration. Drasksel, however, insisted that the Christian religion should be a matter of new life and joy in the Holy Ghost. He was, therefore, silenced. But the break came in spite of repression. In 1767, at Isaac Long's huge barn, the Amish, Lutherans, Moravians, Presbyterians, Methodists, Reformed Dunkards, and Mennonites were all represented in one evangelistic service, as was described, "In unity of the faith and knowledge of the Son of God."

It has been noted, by some authors, that various Old Order groups often sought after the church found in the book of Acts, in the Holy Bible.

Chapter Seven
From Then To Now

The man who led the new Old Order Amish, Jakob Ammann, did not leave accurate details of the movement. We do know, however, that the Amish were ordered to leave Markich in Alsace, in 1712. There is sufficient information after the first departure on the ship, Adventure, to now piece together life as Amish. Although they did not want to leave their homeland, there are two time periods traceable for migration, from 1727-1790 and 1815-1860.

At first, the immigrants sailed to Philadelphia and then spread farther north and west through Ohio. They soon learned a better route for infiltrating the western Americas. When some arrivals landed at New Orleans to travel to Illinois, Indiana, and Ohio, the overland trek was abandoned in lieu of the river route. The immigrants had never seen such a fascinating machine as the steam boat; no such transportation existed in Europe. Up the Mississippi the boats steamed. Huge smoke stacks towered above the three story decks. As usual, the poor slept top deck; children on cotton bails when available while adults were wrapped in blankets.

The Ohio River blends into the Mississippi around Cairo, Illinois, and thus opened the new route to Ohio. The Amish finally settled into their new environment. They cooperated as much as possible with those in authority, although the time came when public education brought a new cross in the road. With the coming of higher education, the Amish decided not to obey the law of sending children to school up to the age of sixteen. They believed an eighth grade education could suffice any boy or girl on the farm. This was another time of peaceful resistance until some parents lost their children to the court system. It was only a matter of a few weeks, but the Amish drew on their rights as citizens and the children came home. The children were being consolidated into large schools and the Amish were concerned that the secular teachers were not upright, moral people. They feared, furthermore, that children would lose the environment of a farming community. They were taught to care for each other as a community instead of individuals seeking self-propagation. The parents were concerned, also, about the trend toward long bus rides taking time away from home chores and added homework. The secular schools also began to teach evolution, sex education and the use of the television. Because of this, the Amish pay taxes but support their own system of education by patrons and the church. In the year of 1937, one room schools began to appear that were exclusively Amish. Heated by coal or wood, the schools relied mostly on natural daylight to teach and study by.

The Amish, as other cultures and societies, have experienced rebellion among their own. In a Goshen News account, 1951, some young Amish men decided to strip down a buggy for racing at the Elkhart County Fair, in Indiana. The purse was $350 for the winner, which prompted the Amish to declare it gambling. When asked about the incident, one youth announced that the time had come to break some of the strict rules. He also declared, "We'll cope with the consequences later." The Goshen residents said they knew it had to come someday. They named these Amish youth, the yanked-over Amish.

In spite of only going to formal school eight years, the Amish speak three distinct languages; in the United States: High German for reading and reciting the Bible, Pennsylvania Dutch, not to be confused with the language of the Netherlands, and English. Most of what the Amish read is English and most written communication is English, however, church services are in modified High German. Also, still in use today is the oldest known hymn book, the Ausbund Hymnal, which is over 460 years old.

Before leaving the young people, here is a brief note. The Amish enjoy autograph albums. This saying was addressed to Joseph (no last name given).

To My Friend
Long may you live
Happy may you be
Blessed with forty children
Twenty on each knee
Joe Hershberger, Burton, Ohio

The Old Order Amish live in many countries, but all are gone from Europe. In the U.S. they dwell among 20 states and one group in Canada. There are only 126 family names among them. In Indiana and Ohio, the names Miller and Yoder are prominent, with Stolfus and King residing in Pennsylvania.

At this point we have traveled through a brief history, from the Anabaptists beginnings to the year of 2008. It was into centuries old customs and traditions, continuing as the foundation religiously and socially, that David King and Barbara Smoker arrived. How little they knew what the outcome would be when God knocked at their heart's door.

April 1, 2004
Top row, L to R: Amos, Jacob, and Katie
Midle row, L to R: Benjamin, Barbara, David, and Leri
Bottom row L to R: Malinda, Elam, David Jr.

Chapter Eight
Life Is Good

*J*acob and Mary King had settled into an old stone house in Lancaster County, outside Quarryville, Pennsylvania, near route 372. This area is southern Lancaster and considered the most conservative part of the Amish community living there. The house needed remodeling which in time took place. It was cool in summer and at first also cold in winter. The Kings purchased forty acres of land and intended to raise their family on the farm.

Four sons and two daughters brightened the household for Jacob and Mary. David, the oldest boy, arrived at the Lebanon Hospital and was sandwiched between two girls, followed by three brothers. Born November 2, 1960, David and his family had spent five years in Lebanon County where he was born. Jacob and his wife decided a move had to be made because of the then existing spiritual environment for their youngsters. The Kings desired a more conservative place which they found in Lancaster County, the second largest Amish community in the States. Jacob was a strict parent keeping conflict at a minimum for his household. A hard worker, he added a dairy barn with twenty head of cows, horses for plowing, and several more buildings that housed a buggy shop and a hen house. Daily chores started early for the Kings, therefore, breakfast came after the earliest chores.

It required five or six people to milk the cows morning and evening. No machines were used for milking, so the children learned this task and many more at an early age. However, the bulk tank used to store milk had a diesel engine which ran a compressor to cool the milk.

Spring was an exciting time for David. The sound of song birds trilling their choruses quickly announced the change of season. The pasture now became green and inviting for the cows. To watch them run and frolic over the grass was comparable to how the family felt after being closed in all winter. Soon ground breaking time arrived which meant shoes and socks could be discarded until autumn. David loved to push his bare feet through the grass cooling them while the sun rose high overhead. Then the family began to plant the seed that brought a luscious crop of hull and snow peas in early spring. Ears of corn both field and sweet, later appeared on the stalk and work began in earnest. Farming produced plenty of healthy foods to laden the table every meal and Jacob and Mary worked diligently to supply the best for six healthy appetites. Mary King, David's mother, was an industrious person. She had several garden plots near the house that produced a variety of foods as well as brightened the landscape. Warm of heart and disposition, she taught David to work his own garden plot. Thus the boy learned the art of producing a variety of food. Mary shared the seed catalog with her son and they looked for new crops to try. David found a yellow raspberry that was sought after for its fresh, sweet meat. He played the gardener wisely by copying Mary's example. Even though farm life was rigorous and filled with hard work, it was a rewarding life.

After the early peas, it was berry picking time and June passed quickly for David. A favorite type was the Sparkle Strawberry. Red, plump, and juicy, the customers lined up in front of the King's vegetable stand to buy their share. Living near a major road helped the sales; enticing people from a long distance to the farm. When picking time arrived, several teenaged girls were hired to help. David was included in this adventure and enjoyed the brisk pace of work. The berries were often gone while orders still lingered. Jacob constructed wooden carriers to load the berries on for transportation to the stand and even with so much help and activity, customers were obliged to wait or return for purchases. Two more fruit types appeared around strawberry season. Cherry trees that grew along the fence rows and mulberry trees, especially one large tree near the edge of the field, always produced a good harvest. David anticipated the fun of rough and tumble tree climbing. The dark red, luscious cherries were worth the work, but climbing the mulberry tree was best. Large sheets of plastic were spread under the limbs to catch the treasures. A few folk had to watch with envy while only one scrambled up, limb by limb, to reach just the right spot to give the tree a good shaking. Some twenty to thirty gallons were retrieved, often as large as a child's thumb. This inviting treat was consumed as often as the children liked. Purple mouths, purple tongues! Mary extracted juice from this crop to be canned for winter consumption when snow would fly.

As the sun rose high in the bright summer sky, the golden heads of wheat drooped over, laden with glistening grain. It was harvest time in the field. One farmer usually owned a binder and pulled it from farm to farm with four to six men helping each other. This was especially exciting for the boys involved. The machine made quick work when the wheat was cut, automatically bound and popped the bundles into the field. Time after time the boys hoisted shocks up to lean against each other; this enhanced the drying time and helped rain to run off. Amish children learned early on how to make a game out of work. Outstretched arms eagerly reached forward as men tossed the ready bundles upward into the wagon. Who worked the fastest? They soon found out. Next, the hum of the threshing machine turned to clatter as bundles were run through to automatically separate grain from straw. Here the baler created straw bales, great for animal winter bedding. The next session of labor left row on row of hay covered ground. The engine driven, hay mower traversed the field leaving cut hay to dry a couple of days. The workers breathed in the sweet aroma as they raked it into rows. Here the baler was a two person operation. One drove the horses to propel the baler while another perched atop the wagon to stack bales as they came up the shoot A fully loaded wagon made its way to the barn. By this time an elevator was employed to stack it all.

Amish boys, as others, used innovation to create games. The bales, about one and a half feet in height and width, and three feet long, served perfectly when stacked into a maze. Plenty of room for makeshift dwellings or dens, or whatever resulted. But Sunday was different. Amish communities hold church service only twice a month, thus every other Sunday was family time. Often times, the Kings struck out for a walk in the woods. Here the uplifting fragrance of wildflowers wafted on a gentle breeze, brought much relief from the heat of the day. Summer moved at a fast clip with so much to be finished before autumn set in. But time slips away and the ladies canning sessions now slowed and autumn would not wait. With the advent of summer behind them, autumn meant a return to school with studies and cherished friends.

David reluctantly put his shoes back on for the two mile trek to their one room Amish learning center. A teen-aged girl was often the teacher for about thirty pupils. Classes ran from first grade through eighth. Although Amish children never took part in sports such as football or basketball, they excelled in a form of baseball for exercise and pure enjoyment. David was especially good at reading but another "r" word was his specialty. Much leg work at home gave him strength to compete well in running. He excelled in this part of recess. An exciting game was under way when David picked up his bat and stepped up to the plate. He leveled his eye and bat just right. Off into the blue sky streaked the ball, its flight cheered on by the spectators. As David rounded the field cheers went up, "Run, David, run. You did it!" He plowed into home plate! Home Run! And what could be better than a reward for hard work. David took a teacher's challenge to memorize the beatitudes.

"Blessed are the poor in spirit..."

"Blessed are they that mourn..."

It wasn't easy but he remembers them even as an adult.

Of course, a change of leaves did not stop work that needed to be completed at home. Corn husking awaited and soon a wagon, sides added high above, was pulled by two sturdy horses sensitive to their job. At first the walk through rows of stalks needed only a "stop" or "go" to direct the horse's path but soon the shuffle of shoes and the sound of voices coaxed them to move forward, even while corn bounced into the wagon. The corn crib was filled now with winter feed. Men from the feed mill in town came from time to time to transport the corn to the mill for grinding. After salt and minerals were added for nourishment, the sweet smelling grain was returned.

School was rolling along now and the chill of snowy days lay just ahead. Suddenly, the first flakes of snow danced along the window panes; swooped down among the bare tree limbs to usher in sled and skate processions. Sled tracks found their way over the frozen field as the Kings heralded the first signal of winter. If the ponds froze enough, slipping and sliding on ice brought rosy cheeks and a lot of laughs.

Even though winter provided the children with some activity, David still had a love for his books. His studies turned into a lifetime hobby of reading with his favorite spot being near the woodstove in the living room. Thus David passed his young years and into his teens, contented with life on the farm. When he reached young adulthood, his decision to be baptized into the Amish faith and also to become an organic farmer was realized. David's mother played an important role in his religious training. She took him to church at the very beginning of his life, six weeks old and it continued on from there.

Jacob, David's father, was well established as an organic farmer and was the influence on his life to follow suit. For David King, life was sometimes difficult when family worked hard to make ends meet but he still felt the farm was the best place to spend his life.

Chapter Nine
A Contented Life

The trees had turned their own respective colors; gold, orange and bronze blazed in the morning sunlight. Amos and Malinda Smoker had two girls and one boy when another baby arrived that fall day. Barbara Smoker was born October 10, 1962 at the Smoker's home in Lancaster, Pennsylvania. The order would reverse after Barbara's birth. Two more boys and another sister followed Barbara. At a young age, Barbara marveled at the sight of pine trees laden with snow; the wash line and meadow fences that glistened with icicles, and even the sound of crunchy snow under foot when dad, Amos, and helpers stomped on the porch, as they came in for breakfast. The winter sky that hosted star light and the perfect whiteness of the moon all told her that God was real.

A wintry wind whistled around the three story brick house the Smoker family called home and rattled windows of this haven. The place was large and roomy with several living areas on the first floor. Her parent's bedroom, the kitchen, a parlor, bathroom, and wash house plus the butcher shop took up the entire first floor. On the second floor, the three brothers shared two rooms, while a large room with two double beds sufficed for the four girls. Bedrooms were not a place for play time; the spacious kitchen served that purpose. This was the place where family ate, worked, and relaxed together. A guest bedroom occupied part of the second floor, also, and several rooms for storage. In the top floor, an attic; old magazines, diaries, and records found a home, while under the structure, a cold cellar was created for can goods and potatoes.

The kitchen was the only truly warm room when Ol' Man Winter arrived. The farm came alive at four o'clock every morning when Amos stoked the kitchen fire and made his way out to tend the livestock. By five o'clock, alarms shattered the dream world of Barbara and siblings. It was a rushed session to dress and hurry downstairs to warm the body, but the smiling faces of their parents always warmed the heart. A hot, welcome breakfast awaited them after the first chore was completed; that was milking. Two or three youngsters assisted Amos in this task. They soon learned the temperaments of each animal and called them by name. Daisy, Rosie, and Dolly all wore various patterns of black and white, however, Dolly was the cow left to Amos for milking. Her short temper and habit of kicking set her apart from the gentleness of the others. The sweet odor of hay, contented cows, and a song hummed by her dad made this one of Barbara's favorite tasks. Even when spring arrived, the farm schedule revolved around the milking; one reason the family retired early.

Amos proved to be a thrifty manager. He raised extra beef cattle and hogs to sell without making a heavier work load for his family. As other Amish farmers, Amos raised feed for his cattle while Malinda's gardens burst with fresh vegetables to be canned. It wasn't easy to pay off the land but even the children were willing to mark off store bought items for school lunches to accomplish this. By the time Barbara was sixteen, Amos had remodeled the house and barn.

Winter evenings held close family ties. The steady rhythm of Malinda's peddled, sewing machine blended with small talk while the girls crocheted or embroidered items for their hope chests. A good book was another favorite way to relax on wintry nights. Then, too, there was the pageant of dozens of pheasants that crossed the yard and flew into the neighbor's evergreen grove to roost for the night. Just before the gas lamp was lit, just at dusk, was the best time for Malinda and her girls to catch sight of this wonderful display.

Balmy breezes pushed through the open windows and of course, rain announced the next change of season. Spring thunderstorms usually produced a rainbow and a wonderful mud puddle behind the barn. Barbara was anxious to dart outside and immediately tromp the puddle, squashing mud up over her toes. It was great fun to build a house, or a canal; then to sail a corn husk boat along the water. Along with the colorful gardens of radishes, peas, and lettuce, the Smoker's home itself was perfumed with pine oil wafting from room to room. Malinda Smoker scoured the place spring and fall. On Saturday morning, the whole kitchen was scrubbed with the help of even the little ones. They wiped down benches, tables, chairs, cabinets, windows, and the floor. It was the most used room in the house and a challenge to keep presentable. One of Barbara's first responsibilities she took pride in was a cleaned wash bowl and shiny faucet. She accomplished this alone. Then there were times when Barbara simply wanted to hear her mother sing. She sang a few snatches and soon Malinda joined in. This worked especially well when her mother was sewing. She probably never guessed. Barbara smiled.

One spring, Amos took on the job of teaching Barbara to raise chicks. At the end of March or early April, 25-50 new beaks pecked away at their shells until yellow puffs of babies arrived. The wash-house was home for them until they had grown a little, and it seemed a short time between having the scent of fresh turned earth until purple tops of clover appeared. Gardens were dressed elegantly now and announced loud and clear, summer is here. As others, the Smoker siblings always looked for a way to produce some fun. The game of bird watching was usually won by an older brother who was in the field and had a good opportunity to identify many species.

With no lack for work to be done, grandparents occasionally arrived to help with building projects or canning; this was also a time of storytelling from the cherished grandparents, with little distraction. Fresh vegetable soup and full course meals helped to satisfy the workers palates. A lunch that might include crunchy salad and a ruby red watermelon was a feast for afternoon refreshment, while the fragrance of V8 juice and beans lingered in the summer air. The Smoker siblings felt work with grandparents truly was grand.

With summer on the wind and grass rising high, Barbara helped with lawn mowing, but the task turned into a game. An older sibling pushed the mower and employed younger ones to pull; of course, these were the horses. Another chore Barbara truly enjoyed was to help hang out wash. Her young hands lifted a fresh, clean piece of laundry that was immediately caught by a summer breeze. The clothes pin slipped into place; held it tightly to dry. A whiff of familiar wash soap lingered as she moved down the line. Barbara felt the lift of spirit in a job well done. Still, the children found time for the sand box and swing in the pine tree. On summer nights, the steady croak of frogs and chirp of crickets invited the family out to the porch. Fireflies flashed above the meadow to join the noisy nocturnal creatures and created peaceful times for the family. It would not be easily forgotten.

Here at the farm, urgency sets in when autumn arrives. School begins late August or early September. With the passing of summer heat, cool evenings became invigorating and lent to restful nights. At the end of one busy day, Barbara was welcomed by her comfy bed. But her mind stayed busy with an unwelcome dream. Suddenly, she was on the move; chased by a nest of bees. It was Amos who rescued her with just the right comfort. He knew how to make Barbara feel especially loved and protected.

It was Barbara's mother who loved to watch nature produce its shows. She was equally at home as she observed a storm produce belts of rain or her perceptive eye scanned animals and insects. On one special occasion she called Barbara alongside to observe a locust making its triumphal exit from its shell. Although Barbara's mother was small of stature, she was filled with enthusiasm that spilled over to the children. She constantly encouraged change, especially clean up projects and the organization of the household. Malinda was spiritually perceptive, as well. The Amish have church services every other week, however, Malinda taught her children on off Sundays. She brought out the picture Bible with German print. Then they would begin singing the old hymns in German; Barbara loved it all.

With all the other events that took place, the farm was still the farm, with lots of cats. Besides the delicacy of mice, they grew readily on milk served morning and evening. Even so, Amos set plenty of traps around the barn. Since they were all kittens first, Barbara enjoyed the feel of a furry ball curled around her ankles. Her senses were especially keen to such things as the scent of foamy milk, musty sweet clover hay, fresh ground feed, and chopped green corn silage. Then there was the scrape of her dad's shovel as it made its way through the feed cart or the cackle of banty hens and the crow of a banty rooster perched atop the fence were never missed.

As with many Amish families, a walk in the fields or along the creek together was a treat. However, there were times that Amos and Malinda preferred to rest from a busy work week, so the children considered it a special time when their mother and father walked with them through the leaves arrayed in their crimson and golden hues; while the ear caught the thud of nuts against the carpeted floor. The corn had been husked and school was in session again.

Barbara loved the smell of new books. The three-quarter mile walk to a one room building was not bad until the frosty air bit their nose and stung the toes. Chores were still done with the boys outside while the girls helped prepare a grand meal for supper. Then time travels full circle with a winter wonderland that changed the scene.

The Smoker household was a dwelling of contentment. They never traveled long distances but when the oldest daughter married, trips were made to White Deer Valley in Lycoming, Pennsylvania, some 130 miles away. This new and exciting adventure included traveling in vans and Barbara probably ate her first meal in a restaurant at age fourteen. Thus she grew up to become an Amish young lady who wanted to continue her life on a farm with loved ones and cherished memories. She never conceived the thought of losing any of the closeness of an Amish community. Her life moved on.

Chapter Ten
The Meeting Place

Young Amish people have the benefit of meeting the opposite gender at singings held in homes. Every Sunday evening, the youth gathered usually on a rotation of parent's houses or the home where a service had been held that day. Excitement ran high, for the young Amish realized they just might meet their life's partner at this very event. The age to attend the meetings was set at sixteen years old until upper twenties or marriage. People came from the local church district, but the event extended to include the whole Lancaster County. This arrangement was a rather formal setting with singing that lasted several hours. The young people took turns choosing and leading the old Amish hymns.

The girls rode with brothers and sisters or even a neighbor boy and sister or whoever might be going that way. They traveled in open buggies, pulled by frisky horses that were the pride and joy of the boys. An umbrella served the purpose in rain, comforters for winter, or light dusters in summer. The long rides turned into fun sharing times. This is where David and Barbara first met. He was eighteen and Barbara sixteen. Thus a friendship sprang into being as they noticed favorable traits about one another. Barbara took note of David's kindness toward his sister. She was to learn later how he kept his peppy horse in top condition, and of course, David had dark hair and was handsome. As for David, Barbara's special smile and modesty attracted his attention. She didn't extend herself or bring attention to herself. So began a friendship that became a courtship. David asked Barbara if he could take her home as a special friend. Two years later; at ages 22 and 20, David and Barbara decided they wanted their relationship to continue on permanently. They were right for each other.

Amish weddings are very different from the common sort. They begin at 8 a.m. and take in the entire day with much preparation before this grand occasion. Since the event is to be the beginning of a lifetime together, great measure is taken to ensure the best for the couple. The bride's mother prepares all summer for every detail. Extra food is grown and chickens are raised especially for the roast. Then there is the fixing up of the old home place with a new coat of paint. Often new clothes are sewn for the entire family. The entertaining of the groom's parents occurs while no expectation of work intrudes upon them. It is normal for three hundred or more people to be present for a grand celebration.

The bride's mother makes certain that all jobs are listed with certain people to handle them. Four married couples cook the roast, another four couples peel, cook and mash by hand, bushels of potatoes. Assorted groups wash dishes and someone, usually an elderly aunt, hangs the dozens of dish towels out to dry. Two meals are served, one at noon and another in the evening. Assigned persons serve the food and yet others clean up afterward. The Amish consider a person's action of taking on these public responsibilities to show how well they are willing to cooperate and even makes a statement of who that individual is.

In Lancaster County, it is an old tradition for weddings to be held in the fall. David and Barbara decided on Thanksgiving Day, November 25, 1982 for their date. It was a typical November morning about twenty degrees, bright and sunny. By afternoon, the weather had warmed up nicely. The immediate church family, along with relatives and friends made up the group of about three hundred. The couple enjoyed their special day as couples had for generations.

Barbara's home was set up for the wedding. The bridal party sat in the center of the place. The first event was a service with two preachers participating. They traveled from Genesis to the New Testament centering on passages of scriptures based on marriage and the home. In the forenoon, wedding hymns were sung and the actual ceremony performed by David's uncle, Israel Beiler. Another song was sung before the house was completely rearranged to accommodate eating. Temporary tables were fashioned out of benches supported by tresses or saw horses. Tables lined the walls and workers stepped up to serve the traditional meal. The young people had a special place along with the newly wedded couple. The afternoon continued on until the second meal was finished. The Amish love to sing. As people began to drift away, the singing went on until about ten p.m. The day was finished; the wedding was over.

Chapter Eleven
Barbara's New Beginning

After Barbara and David's wedding, Jacob and Mary took on the task of building furniture and getting the other end of the house ready for the couple to move in. Barbara and her mother refinished furniture and made comforters, blankets, and quilts. The winter passed and by early spring David's green house was producing new seedlings. Barbara was busy, also, working in the produce patch and selling at the stand. She was especially glad that David worked at home and allowed them to work as a team. David was a wonderful help with the responsibility of each new baby that arrived. Also, his parents became very precious to her; especially David's mother, Mary, who helped answer Barbara's many questions on cooking, canning, and sewing. David's sister, Nancy, also proved to be a blessing when a new name was added to the household. Barbara's mother came as soon as possible to tend her for several days. Barbara became attached to others in David's sphere of life. She still possessed the easy going spirit and kindness that first attracted David to her. She easily made close friends with women from the neighborhood and adopted his church district as her own. But her devotion would always be with her parents, Amos and Malinda Smoker. She enjoyed just being with her dad in the barn while they worked. He was strong, worked hard, and Barbara trusted him to take care of everything. Malinda was small of stature and not physically strong as some, but her enthusiasm carried over to the children. She instigated constant improvement, especially certain clean up projects. So it was a great shock to Malinda, Barbara, and the Smoker family when Amos fell while completing repairs on a barn roof. On that particular day, he had worked alone on the roof project. When he died, they lost their beloved father and grandfather.

Barbara's brother had taken over the farm but Amos was always active. He was found dead near the ladder. This occurred in May of 1999, yet the goodness of the Lord prevailed. Just ten days earlier, Amos and Malinda had come to visit them in Virginia and helped build a new addition to their home. These fresh, precious memories lingered in Barbara's mind; yet before them lay a long journey.

Chapter Twelve
David and Barbara
Starting Out

*D*avid and Barbara started on their round of weekend vis-
its to all the relatives and friends who had been invited to their
wedding. This old Amish custom allowed them to sew pillow
tops, play games, especially jokes, along with quizzes with the
family's children. This was a carefree winter, usually traveled in
open buggies and in the company of other young married couples. Then settling in really began. Jacob and Mary King
enjoyed a large home with a separate living quarters attached.
This is where David and Barbara took up housekeeping for the
first four years of their marriage. Barbara was especially happy
because David was an organic farmer, thus he was able to stay
home. This provided them the opportunity to work as a team. He
was also very much involved when the children made their
appearance.

The family stand was taken over by the young Kings while Jacob continued the dairy business. However, when David's brother married and prepared to take the dairy work, Jacob sold David several acres to build on. Since two little ones had made their entrance into the household, room was now lacking. Jacob arrived July 18, 1984 and Amos two and a half years later. A barn was completed first with the family residence in the top and the animals beneath. Before Katie, the first daughter arrived, they moved into their new home. David had decided in the meantime to sell wholesale instead of retail. No customers to disturb their meals proved to be a good move. Five children were born while they lived in Lancaster. Benjamin and Levi were added to the household before the move to Virginia was made. The little Kings were blessed with a new school by then, just a mile away.

Chapter Thirteen
Search For A New Home

David and Barbara believed they would always be conservative Amish. They believed what they had been taught growing up in the tradition but somehow this couple noticed the trend toward drifting away by many of their people. The ministers and bishops usually were spiritually minded but others, often, were not. David's cousin, Abram Stoltfus and his wife, Naomi, were likeminded. Another couple, Levi and Lizzie Fisher were added to the group. All were organic farmers so they shared many helpful sessions on farming and developed a firm friendship. The three men spent time discussing ongoing incidents they felt important to young families in Lancaster. David readily opened up his feelings to them and in the course of time they decided to search for a new community or move close to an existing one. A turning point came for David while still in Lancaster.

A yearly meeting was held for parents, ministers, and the school board to talk about the coming school year. The decision had been made to eliminate Bible stories from the curriculum. The parents had the opportunity to ask questions or to comment on this concern. When David could speak, he, without hesitation, asked why this could be when their forefathers used the Bible to teach from the very beginning. This was a stand for what he felt was right more than obedience, which was the reputation of Amish tradition. From that meeting David felt he was marked as different. Barbara, however, was still satisfied. Another five years passed before a definite change took place.

David was now seriously thinking about the Amish way. He realized he was on a journey of soul searching. He began to read other religious literature and felt his people dwelt on too many non-spiritual subjects. At this point a seed was sown in David's heart during a service. One minister preached about the good of digging into the spiritual life. This was an unusual sermon in David's present thinking. This seed took hold and David had no option but to move on in his search. Now was the time for Levi, Abram, and David to begin their conquest of finding a new home.

In 1992, the three couples struck out to seek new land. David had met a local man who was a taxi driver for the Amish.

Martin Hershey was a good man and kind to all. He shared books with David and told him of the baptism of the Holy Ghost. David didn't know that Martin Hershey felt it his calling to share spiritual insights with the Amish. David didn't understand all of this but felt Hershey was the perfect one to help in their move. Finally the trek was made in the spring of 1995 to the beginning of a new life in Abingdon, Virginia. Hershey drove the King family the nine hour trip in his van. The bulk of their belongings were shipped by a semi to be delivered at the farm site. The date was April 24, 1995 and David King stood with his family and possessions on the bank of a river that separated them from their home. The other families had arrived about two weeks earlier.

Enough property had been found for the three families in a unique location. The North Fork River Road runs along the North Fork River in Abingdon, Virginia. To cross the river was the next feat for the family. The surrounding neighbors stepped in to accommodate the Kings with equipment to carry all of their possessions over. Then the goodhearted folk brought food to help since they had a late start for planting. In that same summer these people who had become such a blessing, helped build a swinging bridge across the North Fork to the King farm. Martin Hershey made several trips down to visit and brought along books for David. He learned much from his reading that the Amish never taught, such as laying on hands for healing. David still believed a deeper spiritual walk could be found without leaving the Amish community. He continued to confirm in his own heart that a move outside the ranks would not be necessary. He was to learn even more through a local pastor who had befriended the group when they arrived.

Paul White, the pastor of a small Pentecostal church and his wife Linda, had become friends with the Kings. The family was invited to share a Christmas holiday with the Whites and other guests. Among them were John Brown and his wife, Charlene. John Brown was busy with the job of serving David and family the festive meal but Brown was an observant man and made several mental notes about David King. He felt that God had spoken to him to offer David a Bible study, but a negative reaction set in. "Lord, these people separate themselves. How can anybody reach them?" However, David had already visited the White's church and heard more on the baptism of the Holy Ghost. This was explained as evidenced in a person's life when they "spoke in tongues."

David continued seeking Bible knowledge in whatever method he could. Another door opened when David wrote to an author of a book he read. A notation in the book stated that no group was too small for the author to hold a meeting. That intrigued David and a date in March of 1999 was set. He quickly invited the Amish families to the event and some friends from the non-Amish community as well. By this time Barbara's sister Rachel and husband Benuel King had also moved to the area. A group of some thirty people attended, including Paul White. During the service Reverend White spoke briefly on some spiritual matters. Following this, the guest speaker took the floor. At the conclusion, he asked if anyone wanted prayer for healing. Becky Lapp, a young school teacher, who had come from another community, came for prayer. She was instantly healed of a knee problem. Next, Abram's oldest daughter, who had not been able to work in a quite normal manner because of back trouble, was instantly healed. Excitement ran high by now for the group. The Amish had never seen this before. When John Brown heard of the meeting, he immediately contacted David to begin a home Bible study.

The King family had grown by two more children after the move to Virginia. David Jr. and Elam were the youngest when the Bible studies began. With the family gathered around the table, John Brown expounded truths unheard of by the King family. With two little ones to tend, Barbara missed a lot of the teaching, yet something began to develop in their hearts. David had read that baptism, according to the Bible, must be done by immersion. As the study progressed he asked John if this was true. John answered yes. He even emphasized this throughout the scriptures. With a non-Amish visitor giving Bible studies week after week to the Kings, some feelings were stirred elsewhere. David was asked to discontinue the study. Since David and Barbara were taught to think of the community above personal desires, the study was dropped, as David wrote to John Brown, "for now." However, Brown was not easily discouraged. While on a hunting trip, God had warned him that this would happen. There was a bird at the hunting camp the hunters nicknamed, "Camp Robber." The Lord spoke to John that as the bird had stolen his food, some people were stealing David's food. He wrote a lengthy letter to David. He didn't directly say what David should do, but when asked if the study should continue, Brown answered yes. David decided if this was God's will, he would not hesitate.

The studies resumed. By now, David realized his baptism had not been scripturally valid. For an Amish person to be baptized again is to denounce one's standing in the church. Unless the person is willing to recant this action, he is put out or shunned. David had a serious decision to make. He loved his people but wanted God's will above all else. In the course of visiting Paul White's church, David had been seeking the experience of the Holy Ghost baptism. He believed the teaching to be true. While at an evangelistic meeting at the Pentecostal church, the minister invited anyone who desired to have this experience to come for prayer. David responded. He was not disappointed. He received a glorious experience and spoke in languages he had never learned. God knew exactly what David needed for encouragement. Now the time had come for real strength. The next step must be taken.

In January, 2000, visitors came to the King's farm. Some were Amish who had left the faith to join another movement. They also had a leader of this group along. It was after much discussion that David decided the time had come for baptism by immersion. David and the leader walked to a cold, snow sprinkled pond to put him under. David came straightway out of the water shouting and rejoicing, for he believed he had obeyed God. David exclaimed, "The fire of God fell on me." David couldn't remain silent about his experience and soon the Amish community heard, but the bishop was especially disturbed. Again, a prophecy had preceded this that assured David God was leading him. Now, more than ever, the Bible study was nourishment for David King.

The people prayed for them to be able to have children. God gave them their desire and this raised the question that took root in Barbara's mind...

Chapter Fourteen
Questions on Both Sides

The move to Virginia to begin a new Amish community was neither well thought of nor supported wholeheartedly by the Lancaster group. The parents and families questioned the motive for "going off by themselves." They reluctantly and sadly helped pack the belongings and saw them off. The three families sought a deeper spiritual fulfillment and without an ordained minister to preach or the usual services, the hunger deepened. David and Barbara felt far away from the people in Pennsylvania; thus they needed a greater relationship with their God. The move brought about a partial separation for them. But encouragement had come before this. When Bennie was born several years before, a very helpful midwife had encouraged them in the Lord. They now expanded their family devotions with more time to read the Bible together, morning and evening, children on laps and close around. Barbara felt this promoted family closeness besides the usual prayers. She had some questions herself by this time.

In 1989-90, a young couple of close acquaintance whom the Kings enjoyed being with, was banned from the Amish church. Since the two couples were of the same occupation, they shared information and learned from each other. The pair had been married for some time before David and Barbara, but was childless. They were humble, quiet and likable people.

The excommunication was a result of some spiritual happening. But the Amish were not to talk about it, in fact, just accept that the bishop had done the right thing. This couple attended a church where faith was exercised. The people prayed for them to be able to have children. God gave them their desire and this raised the question that took root in Barbara's mind. "Why didn't we Amish pray for them?" David and Barbara felt their heartache as they watched the couple in such an awkward position in the bann. But they did not visit as freely as before. It was about two years after the first families settled in Virginia that Barbara's sister arrived. Her husband Benuel King was Naomi Stoltfus' brother. Now two families enjoyed closeness to relatives.

Even though the Lancaster community questioned these moves, occasionally a vanload of family and friends came to spend a few days. There were days of intensive labor with land to be cleared; gardens planted, fences built for horses, cattle and goats. The neighbors brought sacks of beans and rice to help supplement the late start of canning. Even when Christmas arrived, presents arrived also because the Amish were away from their loved ones in Pennsylvania.

Christmas was always special, but for Barbara it was the songs. Her earliest memories of the Christmas season were times of wonder and joy mixed with anticipation and secrets. Homemade cards were created and Malinda told the beautiful story of God's love. They gathered at a grandparent's house for dinner. Uncles, aunts, cousins, brothers, sisters, all met to sing and exchange gifts and treats. It was togetherness that made holidays special and Christmas still meant love and fond memories for Barbara.

Brown Family L - R
Erica, Charlene, John and Amber top center.

Chapter Fifteen
John Brown and Search for Truth

In the summer of 1999, John Brown began his weekly Bible studies. He arrived around 7 p.m. and the family gathered around the kitchen table. Since Barbara had little ones to take care of, she considered this David's Bible study. Bennie oftentimes helped her tend the children so the others wouldn't be disturbed. David, Jacob, Amos and Katie learned quickly. Barbara didn't miss the amazing supply of personal stories that John told of how God moved in his life and the lives of many others. These things intrigued the family and at times Barbara was frustrated because she wanted to listen. She wondered what John meant about "finding out who Jesus is." He also taught on subjects she doubted they should listen to, especially the children. Barbara also realized full well the consequences a non-Amish Bible teacher might cause. They didn't talk much openly about it. The Kings knew a time to grow stronger was needed before any opposition arrived. Their hunger for God was real but they truly didn't know if the direction was right. Month after month, John Brown invested much time and effort into the study. Barbara felt the investment was in the family. She often wondered what John received from all of this. He drove a half hour and traveled through all kinds of weather. His trek included the swinging bridge and trudging a muddy path to the farm. At times, unforeseen situations changed the schedule and he drove out for nothing. One time a van of Amish dropped in during the Bible study time. John packed up and quietly left. As time went on the Bible study became a regular event of anticipation for the children. They would ask, "Is this John Brown day?"

But there was a price to be paid. David and his family were no longer part of the Amish community. They had been banned. They first visited Christian Life Center in Kingsport, Tennessee, in July, 2000. It was an hour away and John picked them up in the large church van. These were difficult times for Barbara. She had been taught to obey her parents, elders, and her husband. The relationship between her family, friends and elders was now a terrible strain. Who could she trust? David and Barbara had already understood another Bible truth. Baptism was to be done in Jesus name by immersion. The Amish baptism was pouring water over the head, using the term, "In the name of the Father, and of the Son, and of the Holy Ghost." David and

Barbara dearly loved their families and friends but they realized they had to please God first.

This Swinging bridge is our "connection", since the river is
between us and the road. We cross it with express wagons of
produce going out. And with green house supplies
and family needs coming in.
Malinda - March 2008

Chapter Sixteen
After Baptism

$\mathcal{D}$avid felt confident that he had obeyed God's will about his baptism in January, 2000. When news reached the Lancaster County community, a storm broke on the horizon. Letters arrived in short order urging him to repent of this doing. However, the criticism only galvanized David's resolve to follow his heart. David's friends, Abram and Levi, now also felt they could not be in good standing with their community and still associate with the Kings. He had tried to explain Biblically why he chose these actions, but tradition and long standing teaching in the Amish faith overshadowed their personnel choices. Abram and Levi eventually admitted that God was not moving in the Amish church as He was in the Pentecostal realm. David felt crushed in spirit to lose this friendship. He reasoned all this out because his own past teaching could have stopped his decision to change. David's strength and faith were sorely tried at this point. He felt God had called him to the wilderness. Barbara was not ready to begin attending non-Amish churches so the Bible studies were all David had for the time.

Levi and Abram made a trip to Lancaster in May, four months after David's action of being rebaptized. They met with the bishop in charge of the community. Several weeks later, David received a notice that a number of leaders would visit Abingdon to see what could be done about David's decision. A service was held at Benuel and Rachel's home on June 25, 2000. A group of five bishops, another five ministers, and a couple of deacons arrived. David and Barbara had attended services and had been involved for twelve years in the Quarryville area where several of these people came from. The Kings had discussed the possibility of the bann. They knew they could not stay for the traditional meal should that happen. John Brown, in the meantime, spent extra time with the Kings and tried to encourage them. He wanted to be present for David's hearing but wasn't allowed. Barbara was the one who felt the importance of remaining with the Amish traditions. David, on the other hand, would not remain Amish at any cost. His mind was made up before any hearing was held.

June 25, 2000 first began with rain, but by the time service ended, the children were dismissed. A member's only meeting was then conducted by an Amish bishop. David was asked
to sit in front with the ministers. He was nervous but prayed for
help. As the meeting progressed, a calm spirit enveloped him,
and David sensed it, for God gave him good answers for the
many questions. All twelve ministers and deacons asked about
his actions. They also questioned many of his choices in preced-
ing months. The elders tried to convince him to confess his
wrong and to back down. Instead, David tried to explain scripture to them and offered them literature. He felt it was a game
of twelve to one.

At the end of almost two hours of questions and answers
the bishop gave the judgment of his case. David was not sur-
prised. All of his life he realized that any person could be
banned. It was part of the Amish way to discipline a wayward
member. It was the Ordnung; the way of life. The bishop began,
"David, you have been stubborn and rebellious. You have not
allowed yourself to be reasoned with. I now pronounce the bann
over you. I Corinthians 5:4-5 states, 'In the name of our Lord
Jesus Christ, when ye are gathered together, and my spirit, with
the power of our Lord Jesus Christ, to deliver such an one unto
Satan for the destruction of the flesh, that the spirit may be
saved in the day of the Lord Jesus.' You were given peace in the

Amish church, and now in the name of the Lord, that peace is being taken away from you." Thus David was officially excommunicated from all in the Amish church. The bishop proceeded, "There can be no eating, no gift exchange, no acceptance of a ride, no financial dealing and no one can accept anything from David's hand." David and Barbara left for home while the rest ate the traditional meal.

Since it was over, the bann in place, the meal finished; the elders stopped by the Kings upon leaving. A deacon stood at the door desiring to talk to Barbara, however, David refused to allow him to remind her of the bann. Barbara had collapsed on their bed in exhaustion. David had many mixed feelings by now. He felt it truly was over. However, God was yet working to bring help. John Brown had so wanted to be with David, but could not. He planned to be with them as quickly as possible. He pulled up to the swinging bridge. The instant his gaze fell upon the river, it seemed especially muddy that day. "So have the eyes of the Amish bishops been muddy today." John knew God was telling him that David was banned. The bishops were leaving when Brown arrived. He cordially shook hands with each one. Only one person refused his hospitality. Brown crossed the bridge expecting to see a downcast friend, but David bounded up and down with joy. "I'm free! I'm free!" was the shout of victory from David's heart. David knew he could never confess to being wrong. His conscious was clear and his punishment was not scriptural. So it was that John Brown told the Kings of a large spiritual family they had not as yet met. He began to bring along one or two people for the Bible study.

Barbara had become ill after David's excommunication. She was just up and about when Brown brought former pastor James Tharp to the house. He immediately talked to her about the infilling of God's Spirit. While Barbara was interested in this experience, she needed something in the physical realm just then. As the little group gathered around her, Tharp felt led to pray for her healing. Not knowing what was wrong, Tharp prayed in earnest. Barbara experienced a new spiritual depth as she was miraculously healed. God also provided in James Tharp the much needed sense of security Barbara so needed. What would God do next for the King family?

The dream of finding more spiritual truth and the presence of God had not evaded them, however, it could not be found within the Amish traditions.

Chapter Seventeen
A Community No longer

The Amish families in Abingdon obeyed what they had been taught for generations. The hope for a real community faded into obscurity after David's bann. They immediately planned to move since no other families would now join them. Barbara's sister and family left for Park County, Indiana about one month later. In obedience to the Amish elders they could not allow David to help them with that task. On one occasion, Abram remarked about a strange fire that was now present.

Letters continued to pour in from family and friends. David desired to answer them with scripture for their better understanding. Thus he readily accepted help from John Brown and James Tharp. The context was the King's obedience to God rather than to the traditions of men. In July, the Kings were very encouraged by a visit from Martin Hershey. While they discussed how to spend the evening, Hershey offered to take them to the Kingsport church. It was a mid-week service and they already knew they would arrive late. Besides this, to visit a non-Amish church still bothered Barbara; however, John Brown had been notified of their coming, so the trip had to be made. The service was in progress when the group arrived. Brown was waiting outside for their arrival and this impressed Barbara very much because she knew no Amish would miss any part of a service to greet latecomers. After a warm welcome, Hershey and the nine Kings filed into the auditorium. This was a first time occurrence for Pastor Keith Barker and flock. The entire experience was a bit overwhelming for the new family. Worship was lively and musical instruments were used. There would be no turning back now because the whole family was involved in learning more about Acts 2:38, the central scripture for Apostolic believers. That is; what the Apostles taught and preached. The Bible study soon bore fruit.

Amos was especially intrigued by Brown's Bible, which was filled with notes and references. He sat close by in the study but it was Jacob, the oldest boy, who announced his desire to be baptized in Jesus name. This was the catalyst for Barbara to make a return visit the following week. Brown offered to pick them up and thus began a yearlong trek to help the family. Although David had his personal Pentecost at Pastor White's church, he was not totally familiar with the worship. He had, however, thought about the event of his January baptism. By the time Sunday evening rolled around David had made up his mind to go to the water again. In January, the preacher had included the term, "In the name of the Father, Son, and Holy Ghost." David now realized his baptism must be based on how the early church performed it. Brown had urged Barbara to obey the Bible baptism; so three candidates were ready on Sunday evening. After the service, Brown baptized Jacob and he came up straightway out of the watery grave speaking in tongues. The presence of God's Spirit descended mightily upon them. Next James Tharp baptized Barbara who was willing to follow. Brown then plunged David beneath the water in Jesus name. A sacrifice had been offered to God and He readily accepted it. David's bann had driven the Kings closer to Jesus Christ than ever before.

All of this excitement took place September 3, 2000, just three months after the bann. By this time Barbara's desire to experience her personal Pentecost rode a high wave. She still was not comfortable going to a non-Amish church on a regular basis, but God had touched Amos and because of this, another trip to Kingsport was planned. Besides, Reverend Tharp was going to preach and Barbara was fond of this new friend. He had helped greatly in the task of seeing that the Kings were well grounded in their new faith. The van rolled up North River Road with John Brown and his family as hosts for the newcomers. The children were caught up in the scenario by this time. They had met more members of this new church family and felt more comfortable this third time out. Amos was baptized on September 17th. It was three months later on December 17th that Amos and Barbara received the Holy Ghost.

Eleven-year-old Katie joined the family of Pentecostals in water baptism January 14, 2001. She too received the Holy Ghost, May 27th. Another birth took place, sandwiched between all of these exciting events. Malinda, David and Barbara's last arrival, was born April 1, 2001. She arrived in time to lift any remaining clouds. The sun shone through all the heartache and hurt to light the sole Abingdon Amish family's journey. However, this was a short respite. God had prepared the couple well for the next letter from the bishop.

Barbara's baptism was noised abroad in Lancaster and she was summoned to a hearing. Barbara exchanged letters with the elders to ask the purpose of this. The result was she refused to go. The next correspondence informed her of her ex-communication. Barbara searched her heart but found no remorse of wrongdoing and had no confession to make concerning a charge. By now no Amish ties remained.

What had begun as a small community of Amish believers no longer existed. Abram and his family had moved to Wisconsin and Levi left for Indiana in April of 2001. David and Barbara had traveled a long road from Lancaster County April 24, 1995 to this point in time. The dream of finding more spiritual truth and the presence of God had not evaded them, however, it could not be found within the Amish traditions.

In 2002, plans were in the making for a Pentecostal church in Abingdon. Until this time David had not thought of owning a vehicle. John Brown had been their benefactor for transportation to church. With the advent of a church in the same town, the Kingsport church family decided to give the large fifteen-passenger van to David. For David, a new adventure began. He soon had a permit and was doing the unimaginable; driving. What a multitude of memories rode along with him every day.

The next blessing occurred when Robert McCann and his wife opened the first prayer meeting on February 18, 2002 in Abingdon. The Kings were present as was the Brown family. Twenty-two pioneers were in attendance and God answered their prayer. They rented the Veterans of Foreign Wars building and held their first worship service. The crowning event was

Benjamin King received the Holy Ghost experience. That Sunday, John Brown baptized him at the Kingsport church.

So it came to pass that the Kingsport church, Christian Life Center, nurtured and established the David King family in a new and totally unexpected transition from Amish to Apostolic. James Tharp, the former pastor of the church, was instrumental in gaining their confidence. The present Pastor, Keith Barker, extended hospitality and wisdom in dealing with the Kings. The Amish community, lost to the Kings, could never be replaced. Their roots reached back to Europe four hundred years previous. Even so, God in His great mercy laid a strong foundation for David and Barbara to build upon.

Chapter Eighteen
Barbara's Turn

*T*he Amish are taught from an early age to respect their parents, the Amish leaders and for women, their husbands. Barbara was now living in a world totally unfamiliar to her. Nothing was secure anymore. The recent event of David's bann had put a strain on every relationship she had ever known. She fully believed David was attempting to follow the will of God. But as a person who suffers from a terminal disease may reach a stage of denial, she too continued to live in denial. Since David's baptism in January of 2000, in the pond, her world had turned into a nightmare.

When the church elders arrived in June for the hearing, Barbara already knew she could not shun her husband. Barbara loved David and her children above all else in the world. She even reasoned with herself that shunning only happened to bad people. She feared being labeled as "disobedient." The Amish way was the hope and desire of her heart for her family. Barbara cherished her parents, David's parents, and the many friends she had treasured. She desired to please all of them but knew that this was impossible.

The hearing had borne fruit in Barbara's heart almost imperceptibly. David answered the questions with a calm assurance without a flinch. She watched him answer the accusations before the entire congregation without recanting or remorse for anything he had done. She decided that only the experience David had received at Pastor White's church could be the answer. David had been filled with the Holy Ghost just as the book of Acts states. He refused to compromise his stand to remain in the Amish church or community. David had desired to remain with them, she surely knew, but could not. He was now shunned. She was expected to fulfill that role also, but knew it was impossible.

The entire extended family was greatly stirred up against his rebaptism. Many of them traveled from Pennsylvania to Virginia to convince him of his wrong. They reminded him of honoring his people who were now grief stricken. Barbara was so torn and hurt for them. She questioned whether David was after all, headed in the right direction. Could all the Amish be wrong about this? Letters arrived that reminded them in great detail concerning the unity of the community. The Amish believe ones individual desires are to be sacrificed for this important trait. Barbara's conflict intensified after the bann, becoming a physical threat. Her pillow was soaked with tears night after night. Who could she trust? Elders? Parents? Her husband? Her body ached from head to foot. Her heart broke emotionally as well as her body. Nothing made sense. She feared displeasing God in a greater measure than all the rest. Barbara longed for just one true friend to stand beside them and to strengthen them. She was so tired of debate and wished just for peace and love to cover her. The core of her being was surely unraveling.

People came and went. John and Charlene Brown both visited and prayed with the family. This brought a measure of peace and warmth into the home. Brown taught David to place his hands on Barbara's head to pray daily for her mind. He also prayed to plead the blood of Jesus over her thoughts and body. She felt uplifted by this process. During this time of wrestling with decisions, Barbara felt a hand touch her. It carried a warm flow of love that encouraged her and assured her God cared personally for her. By this point in her struggles, Barbara realized she really did want more of God.

It was at the end of the first week of David's bann that Barbara was able to sit up on the sofa. Brown brought Reverend Tharp and Larry Boggs to visit. Tharp was the former pastor of Christian Life Center in Kingsport, Tennessee. He reinforced many points for Barbara that Brown had taught in the Bible study. Tharp seemed a strong pillar in the ways of God, which reassured her hunger for truth. Besides this, Tharp reminded Barbara of her precious father who had now been gone for about fourteen months. She saw stability and order in someone once again. Reverend Tharp was quickly adopted in spirit to be Barbara's new grandfather. God worked a direct connection between the two hearts and she felt she could freely express her desire to receive her personal Pentecost. The friends and family then gathered around Barbara to pray for her experience in the Holy Ghost. God directed Tharp to pray for her healing. When Tharp's hands touched her head, a warm flow of God's Spirit radiated over her. She knew this was a healing virtue for her physical and emotional needs. Doubts and fears took flight. A gentle cleansing washed her mind of shattered dreams and then spread down into her innermost being. Barbara realized this instant healing was an act of God, personal and real. For the first time Barbara recognized God's way to work His will for her family. Faith took hold in her heart; confidence for God's protection and guidance multiplied quickly and greatly. Fear of losing the family to the world had tormented Barbara. That dreadful fear was destroyed. Barbara did not as yet experience her Pentecost, but she knew God had supplied her most urgent need, emotionally and physically.

The family's first trip to a non-Amish church occurred when Martin Hershey visited again and wanted to go to church. So the hour-long trip was made to Christian Life Center where John Brown and Reverend Tharp attended. Brown then hoisted little Elam up in his arms to lead the procession into the sanctuary. Barbara felt so out of place in this type of church setting. Here was a modern building, bright, beautiful lights, fine furnishings, and bold blue carpet. Instantly she thought the people lacked reverence for God. The music and people were strange indeed. Amish are taught to be quiet and to listen to the service conducted by the ministers. Here people sang, clapped, and made a lot of noise. And in the church at that! It all was a distraction for her. The thought, "Does God really want everything so modern and fancy," slipped through her mind. "Would He want so much money spent on a building and for whose glory? Don't missionaries need the money more?" She could hardly accept the fact that they were actually in such a modern church. Regular attendance to service was important to the Amish and developed strong habits for them. How would this turn out?

The King family needed a strong support group at this time. A community of friends had been lost; which included family members. Of course, the loss included the friends of the children, also. The whole family felt the rejection very keenly. Barbara quickly learned a healing process made its way into their hearts during the worship service. David and Barbara were reaching for new goals while seeking a way to mend the crushed pieces of a past life. After a few services Barbara was more comfortable, with less concentration on the surroundings. After her experience of repentance, Barbara was baptized in Jesus name. Since her trust had matured she began to make new friends in the congregation, also.

God's presence was very real to Barbara now so regular attendance was a must. The Kings acknowledged that since this group of people had taken them in; the rejection, heartache, and physical needs began to wane as a vapor of smoke. Amos, the second oldest boy, analyzed the situation thus, "The rejection by the Amish actually helped us to seek and embrace the apostolic truth and friendship." They felt as a family, there was nowhere else to go.

When Barbara's initial healing took place, it wasn't until the next day that she noticed her eyes were different, a healing had occurred there as well. She had worn glasses for twenty-five years. As the months passed, Barbara was careful how she spoke of all this to the Amish in Abingdon. But, in the course of time, the news of her baptism reached Lancaster and eventually she received a letter of excommunication. Now she had a goal to be concerned about. She believed the teaching they had received to be true. Healing of the body and mind and the Holy Ghost baptism existed after all. She had started praying, seeking God to finish His work in her life. On December 17, 2000, during a worship service, James Tharp and Pastor Keith Barker felt led to pray again for Barbara's eyes. When Barbara had been prayed for to receive the Holy Ghost in her home, she was healed. Here in the service they concentrated on further healing and suddenly the Lord flooded her soul. Barbara raised her hands in worship and surrendered to God, thanking Him for healing and His love. In the midst of joyous praise, her words suddenly blended together with an unknown language. She had never known anything so wonderful and refreshing. She had "tried" to receive this experience but it had eluded her. It was beyond her understanding. However, when the ministers laid their hands on her, she felt their compassion coupled with God's boundless love and mercy surround her. This was power and excitement for a broken former Amish adherent! It represented the lost security of her father's presence, holding his strong hand as a child to cross a busy street. This new feeling was security in the midst of the storm. God had miraculously transferred the love and respect she held for an earthly father to Reverend Tharp and John Brown. God had finished His work.

Only now could Barbara put her complete trust in Jesus Christ for her family's future. He had provided a path through every circumstance that they had encountered. She felt God made a way when there wasn't any to be seen. Barbara had gained many more brothers and sisters in this church than she had known before. They truly belonged in this family, the family of God.

With many difficult choices behind them, the Kings were unified in their walk with Jesus at long last. Barbara recognized immediately the privilege to be part of this new community. Many friendships were formed in Kingsport, Tennessee by now and Christian Life Center had become the lifeline of nourishment for David and Barbara. The Browns, however, had taught Bible studies for years in Abingdon while continuing to drive to Kingsport. The time was now ripe for Abingdon to reap a harvest. The Kings joined them in praying for a church in Abingdon. Robert McCann was the vessel chosen by the Lord to fulfill the calling. Strong in leadership, especially for the youth, both the pastor and his wife thrived on time spent mingling with the young people. When ten-year-old Jonathon, Pastor McCann's nephew, received the Holy Ghost in the first prayer meeting, the primary group took it as a special confirmation from God. The long night was over. Barbara had met, in person, the Almighty, the Ancient of Days, the Bright and Morning Star, all in one combination and being; Jesus Christ. She could move on at last.

On April 1, 2001, God blessed Barbara with Malinda, Katie's only sister. Malinda's arrival represented, to the King family, the beginning of their new life in Christ. Joy returned to their household a hundred fold. There would be no turning back for the former Amish family. They had gone from Amish to Apostolic in two years.

Celebrating the Holidays with the Brown family.

Chapter Nineteen
Amish Bible Study
John Brown's Testimony

*I*t was Christmas, 1998, when I met the King family. We had gathered for food and fellowship at a mutual friend's house, Paul and Linda White. The Whites were ministers at a local independent apostolic church. David King, the father of the family, shared a sofa with me while we ate. David kept an eye on his children. He quickly discerned a cry of distress from other sounds. This left me with a good impression of him. While sitting there, I heard God say, "Teach him a Bible study." I immediately said, "Yeah right," in my mind. I figured no Amish would receive spiritual teaching from an "outsider." In spite of my protests, I could not get this voice out of my mind. I continued to see images of teaching David King a Bible study.

In the spring or early summer of 1999, my wife sent a letter to David telling him about the Bible study. In July, I received a card from the Kings with a date and time to come for the Bible study. Hallelujah! I was ashamed for doubting God's call.

In the beginning, much of my focus was spent preventing any distractions from the Bible study. This included not taking our two daughters along after the first lesson. Also, I usually wore dark pants and a dark blue shirt as the Amish men wear. Everything went on steadily when I put the study on hold for a hunting trip that was previously planned for October. Omer Yoder was a former member of the Amish community and attended the same church as I. We made the trip to Colorado together. We talked a lot about the Kings, but got no elk on that trip.

While in Colorado we were regularly visited by a common bird of the area, the "Camp Robber." The name comes from the bird's habit of taking anything from the camp they can carry. I took several pictures of this bird, one very close-up.

It was a three-day drive back from Colorado. On day two, God said, "David has stopped the Bible study." Omer was driving at the time and I didn't tell him until later. That night I called home to talk to Charlene, my wife. She said she had some bad news. Before she could tell me, I said, "The Kings have stopped the Bible study." She answered yes and asked how I knew. I told her God had told me. I told her not to worry, everything would be all right. Why would God tell me this if He didn't already have a plan to fix it. I left the next day, alone for the remainder of the trip. Somewhere in Kentucky, God brought to my attention the Camp Robber. I said, "Yes, what do you mean?" God said, "Send David a letter and include a picture of the bird. He's been visited by a camp robber."

Around December of 1999, I wrote David a long letter, which included a photo of the camp robber. I told David he had been visited by certain persons, coming as friends (pretty birds), but they were actually camp robbers - stealing his bread (the Word). I related to him the Colorado bird story. After this, I found out his Amish neighbors had pressured him into ending the Bible study.

- Letter to David King from John Brown -

Sunday Nov. 27, 1999

David King and family,

Greetings in the Name of the Lord. I hope all of you had a good Thanksgiving. I miss our meetings. I was going to tell about my trip to Colorado. So I will do it all in this letter instead. We saw about 50 elk the first day but they were too far away to shoot at. We never could get close enough to shoot any elk. It's such big country out there. You can literally see for miles. Things look so close until you start walking toward them. The temperature was 10 to 20 degrees every night. It took me several days to get used to sleeping on the ground in these cold temperatures. We did much walking every day.

We met other hunters who hunt there every year. They said we could not find any elk because of the lack of snow. Usually they have 3 or 4 good snows by mid October and this drives the elk down off the mountains to lower elevations looking for food. Elk don't like to dig in the snow for food if they can move and find it exposed. They eat grass like cattle. We did have a good time and I always enjoy it out west. We saw many beautiful sights and some of God's small creatures.

When I returned home, Charlene gave me the bad news-that you decided to cancel the Bible studies. Actually it did not sur - prise me. The enemy is always interfering with the spread of Truth. The devil hates the message of Jesus name baptism (immersion) and the other teachings this truth brings with it. He will go to great extremes to stop things. He is most subtle, working in ways we do not recognize and through people we will not suspect. And this brings me to a point I would like to make. God spoke to me about all this on my return from Colorado. He spoke to me about David King (and his family) and me and one of those little creatures I saw.

In fact, I have a picture of the little creature and it's included in this letter. He's a very beautiful little bird. They call him a "camp robber." When God spoke to me, he said "camp robbers had come into David King's camp." They would attempt to carry off food-the Word of God-the truth. They would attempt to end the Bible studies. Camp robbers have been with us since the Apostle Paul's time and maybe before that. God then directed me to several scriptures to share with you.

Matthew 10:38

Shows our biggest hindrances will likely come from those closest to us.

Mark 10:29-30

Tells the good news. It will all be worth it.

Philippians 2:9

Says that we should bow at Jesus' name, not to peers.

Galatians 5:7

The Galatians were hindered from obeying the truth by persuasion (peer pressure) of friends.

I Corinthians 10:13

Good news - God will not test you beyond your endurance. He will help you. With Him you will make it. Forsake all others hold to Him.

One thing I noticed about Camp Robbers, they are persistent. They never give up. They showed up every day. They followed me wherever I went. They were pleasant to be around, it was comforting. Nevertheless they are robbers.

David, God has sent many to guide and lead you into more truth. God is loving. He is patient. He has much for you, even spiritual gifts; the supernatural. He's waiting. So am I. If I've been pretty straight and hard in this letter there's a reason. First, there isn't much time remaining. Second, we're both grown men, we don't need to act like we're little children. You've already been through much, leaving Pennsylvania, etc. Third, I'm not straight with you because I hate you, but because I love you. I want for you what God wants for you. He has brought you a long way; He wants to bring you fur - ther. You're on the edge of change. I know you're wrestling with something at this very moment. Fourth, we're praying for you and your family; that you hear God's voice and have the courage to submit to it. You could be the very key to many Amish brethren entering into abundant light-not just truth - BUT ABUNDANT LIGHT; living in the supernatural realm. We love you, David King, and all your family. You are the spiritual leader of your family. You are the priest between God's drawing power and truth and your children receiving more. I believe you will do the right thing, even if it's stressful. I do not consider our friendship over but only at a changing point. I believe I will see you from time to time. Our door is always open. I pray God will strengthen you.

Love,

John Brown and family

In January, 2000, David King wrote saying he wanted to start the Bible study again. Hallelujah, again! David was baptized in the farm pond in January of 2000. By May of 2000, we spent time attempting to steer David away from the growing tendency to chase every charismatic activity. He had a lot of questions. We assured him he did not have to change his Amish lifestyle to be saved, nor did he have to join our church. I knew David's Amish neighbors had put pressure on him about the Bible study. I asked him to set a meeting with them so I could explain what we were doing. On the day of the meeting, I met two of the men at the river crossing. I didn't like the turn of events after our encounter. In my spirit was an assurance that they were not as sincere in finding more of God as David was. They never ventured on to the house for the meeting. This did not surprise me. I had more important things on my mind.

In June of 2000, my wife Charlene and I had a special Bible study about division and family structure. This was an attempt to prepare David and Barbara for the hearing that was pending. Elders from Lancaster County had informed them of a hearing to question David on his rebaptism. David had accepted the possibility of a bann, but Barbara had not. After the lesson we prayed with them to encourage them. I laid my hands on David's head and began to speak in tongues. In a few minutes I prayed for Barbara and she prayed also, out loud. Again God moved and I began to speak in tongues. I found out later that this was her turning point. Barbara felt something she had never experienced before. She decided to stick with David no matter the consequences. Praise God.

By August 2000, word of the King's experience was reaching people and served as a great witness; one especially of Barbara's healing. James Tharp, our former pastor in Kingsport, explained to Barbara about the Holy Ghost experience. In the midst of his discussion, he stopped and said he would like to pray for her. Brother Tharp did not know she was ill. However, he put his hand on her forehead and prayed for her healing. Barbara said she felt something warm inside, the illness was gone. Later she discovered her eyes were healed.

Another milestone occurred in September of 2000 when Jacob, David, and Barbara were baptized in Jesus name at Christian Life Center, Kingsport, Tennessee. This whole affair has been a lesson for me on perseverance. For the first time in March of 2000, I noticed David referred to the Amish as, "they" instead of "our people". At another time Jacob corrected his father when David said, "We are one of them." Jacob responded, "We look like one of them."

The last little King arrived on April 1, 2001, baby Malinda. This event was especially significant for all involved who helped the Kings find more truth. It was especially eventful for Charlene and I. We both adopted little Malinda as "our granddaughter." Two more special events happened in January of 2004. Levi, a younger King son, was baptized and my picture appeared in the Pentecostal Herald with the King family. I never expected to get such recognition for this or any other home Bible study. The Kings were quite well known in apostolic circles by then.

David and Barbara have come a long way. They took their first plane flight to Salt Lake City for a general conference with the United Pentecostal Church International in September, 2004, and Katie King wed Steven Gullion, a young man in Pastor McCann's Apostolic church in November, 2007.

Who could have known what a simple Bible study might produce. I thank God for allowing me to take part in this family's conversion. I am honored though unworthy. Thank you, Jesus. I'm not sure who learned the most, the student or the teacher.

Her whole face lit up with joy; an expression of joy and peace covered her countenance.

Chapter Twenty
Journey Toward Truth
Charlene Brown's Testimony

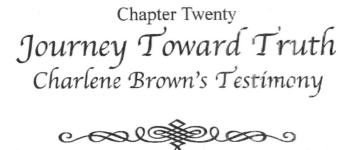

Paul and Linda White pastored the Falls Hill Apostolic Church in Abingdon when three Amish families moved into the area. Our families had been friends for some time, and Linda was the one who introduced us to the Amish.

Our first trip out consisted of Linda, my three children, and myself. We first visited Levi and Lizzie Fisher, and the visit was very memorable, especially since they were harvesting cane for molasses. Several weeks later, we visited the King family.

I told my husband about these families. We were going to the Christian Life Center in Kingsport, Tennessee and knew a young man there named Omer Yoder who was raised Amish. Omer and his wife, Tammy, met us one Saturday to visit the Kings. When we arrived, Barbara was alone with their sick baby boy. In the course of our visit, we told Barbara about a Bible study; Search for Truth. The following week or so, I wrote a letter about the study. However, we never heard from them about it.

Since David was in contact with Linda, she told him he needed to contact John Brown about the same home Bible study. Later John gave them more information about the study and prayed with them. The Bible study then began a week later. The children were well behaved and sat quietly; very attentive. There were so many of them that not everyone could see the small chart, so some of the children had to crowd in to see the pictures. As the study progressed, David sat through it with his arms crossed over his chest and a stern look on his face. Barbara always sat apart in the rocking chair with baby Elam.

At some point the Lord spoke to me to visit Barbara during the day. I had sensed she was struggling with the whole thing and was very uncomfortable. I assured her that we were only coming to their home to teach God's word and nothing more. It was not our intention to change their way of life. One of Barbara's fears was that David would one day own and drive a car. I saw her anguish and did what I could to stifle the fear and assured her as far as we were concerned they were in control of their Bible study and their lives.

During this time they were constantly having visitors from all over the country. One group of visitors came from New York (I believe), and ended up baptizing David in the pond. Barbara was having a hard time accepting this new experience David was coming into. She realized he would be excommunicated from the Amish church and was struggling with this. When the elders did hear of David's rebaptism, they notified him that the bishops were coming to conduct a hearing concerning his misconduct.

David stated that throughout the hearing, the Lord gave him all the answers to every question the bishops asked him. The outcome was his excommunication. David was never shunned by his loving family and they have continued to grow in the Lord. Not long after, on a Wednesday night, a friend from Pennsylvania, Martin Hershey, brought them to Christian Life Center. At the next Bible study, David asked many questions about the church. Their next visit was on a Sunday evening. The family really enjoyed the service. Our retired pastor, James Tharp, began to attend the Bible study with John. He was really overwhelmed at the first visit because the farm reminded him of his childhood on his parent's farm. This immediately formed a bond between Brother Tharp and Barbara. She was bedridden for a week after David's bann. When Brother Tharp prayed for her, Barbara received a miraculous healing. She was up the next day able to do her normal work. It was not long after this that many of the King family were baptized. The service was one of the most anointed services we have had in the years John and I have attended the church. Barbara later received the Holy Ghost. Her whole face lit up with joy; an expression of joy and peace covered her countenance. It brings me tears of joy to know the (before) Barbara and now have the privilege to know the (after) Barbara. No matter how good we are, we still need the wonderful baptism of the Holy Ghost.

I knew Barbara wanted another girl, so when she told me she was expecting, I told her this was incredible; the Lord would give her and David this baby, a new life to parallel their new life in the spiritual realm. I also told her she would have a girl. The day Malinda was born, April 1, 2001, I had the honor of holding this precious baby when she was only thirty minutes old. I told Barbara that John and I would be this baby's grandparents, but it turned out we are grandparents to all eight of the children. When Jacob, Amos, and Katie graduated with GED's, we were there. Jacob went on to graduate with an Associate degree from the community college and we were there.

The weekly Bible studies continued and were completed. It is our prayer that they have learned the things they needed to know about their new life.

We attended a general conference with the Kings and saw the tremendous popularity they have achieved. I like to tease Barbara when we go to a ladies conference that everyone wants to talk to her, but no one cares if they talk to me or not. Since the Bible study has ended, our families remain close and it is such joy to be fellow saints with such a steadfast and faithful family. We spend many holidays with them since we are substitute parents. The Lord always fills our needs with spiritual substitutes. I believe the King family has seen one miracle after another in their new walk with the Lord.

There is so much peace and happiness that can only come through that special connection with Jesus, my Lord. He lives inside me; the Creator of all things lives within my soul. I can call on Him anytime day or night.

Chapter Twenty-One
After Pentecost
- Brother David -

*O*ur manner of life is much the same as before our conversion. We are still farming in Abingdon. The first summer here was much work, clearing land and repairing a run down farm. We learned of the organic farmer's co-op, the Highland Bio-Produce, in Abingdon and soon were selling our produce to them. They sold to stores and restaurants interested in organic products. We continued to focus on that aspect for several years. In 1999, we began selling our goods at the Abingdon Farmers Market. Other Amish families sold there also and sales were fairly good. Besides produce, we had jams and jellies. Then came the berries; strawberries, raspberries, blackberries, and even the minor berries, or less known products such as gooseberries and currants. I had planted one of my favorites again, also, the mulberry trees. Then there is the item of transportation. Sometimes our friends and neighbors helped with transportation;

however, we used the horse and wagon to carry everything to market as well. Since this was a regular occurrence from April through much of November, a manager was needed for the market so when Jacob reached mid teen years in 2002, he acted as the manager. We arrived at seven in the morning and closed at noon. Now Jacob has gone on to other work and I now manage the market again. Thankfully, this market has become one of the best in the area and supplies the greater part of our present income.

Over the years we continued to sell to the Co-Op that had more stores with better outlet though prices were not as good. We also have a friend who runs the Community Supported Agriculture Organization. This is a subscription based means to sell directly to families who want organic products. They receive a basket a week of produce that is in season. They pay in advance, and are a good outlet.

Life on the farm is still the same. We have four horses and in a normal year have enough hay to feed the horses and goat herd over the winter. We have an old fashioned piece of equipment called the hay loader. It picks up hay from rows in the field and drops it onto the wagon. Then at the barn, a pulley is in the very peak of the building attached to a rope. The fork is let down with someone to thrust it into the hay. It grabs the hay, and a horse with rope attached, moves forward, pulling the hay to the top of the hay mound.

After Benuel and Rachel left, we were privileged to farm several acres in that area. The land lies east of us and provided six acres for corn and hay, and ten acres for pasture. This has been a blessing for us. A local, non-Amish couple has purchased the farm and are now remodeling the house. They will move in soon.

Since our farm lies across the North Fork River which separates us from the road, there can be situations of concern that arise. For instance, in March of 2002, the river flooded. The road is estimated to be about fifteen feet higher than the river. The storms were such that water was into the road and over-flowed into the farm ground about one hundred feet. As the current uprooted trees and swept them along, the tops became lodged against the walking bridge. When the force of the river upturned the trees the roots surfaced raising the bridge and allowed it to flop down again. This created major damage to the bridge.

Time moves on and so has our family. Steven Gullion and Katie, our oldest daughter, met and became fast friends at the Abingdon Pentecostal Church where they were married

November 24, 2007. They now live near Abingdon. Jacob has his own apartment and while Amos works away from the farm, he lives at home. Bennie, Levi, David Jr., Elam, and Malinda are home schooled and help on the farm.

The church is our focal point in life. Since its inception in 2002, a steady growth has occurred. We have rented buildings but now have purchased property and begun our building project. Barbara and I still feel the farm has been the ideal place to raise our family. We have worked together, sold together, and have grown together. This, we count as the blessings of God.

This brings me to the spiritual aspect of my life. I would not trade this experience for anything in the world. This is extremely precious to me. Above all else I must be saved. I must be ready for the coming of Jesus for His church. Before I even understood the full plan of salvation, I knew I had to obey. I don't want to come to the end of life and find I didn't make being saved. To spend eternity with Jesus is my goal. Everything I had to go through to arrive to this point in life has been worth it all.

There is so much peace and happiness that can only come through that special connection with Jesus, my Lord. He lives inside me; the Creator of all things lives within my soul. I can call on Him anytime day or night.

We did not make the change from Amish because we wanted a different lifestyle. Most of that is the same. I dress mostly the same. We wanted more of what God had for us. My heart goes out to the Amish who are also searching for more of God. I had a choice to make. The question was: will it be too high a price to pay to follow Jesus all the way? That meant losing family and friends. However, in this truth there is a greater connection with my spiritual family than with the natural. I have thousands of brothers and sisters in the Lord. One of the greatest blessings is that my children are in church and have embraced this wonderful truth. As a family, we have learned the freedom of worship. The Bible tells us to clap our hands and shout with a voice of triumph. As an Amish I never understood this. Now I have the privilege to shout aloud and lift my hands. Praises such as hallelujah and praise the Lord are rendered vocally during worship service.

There is a great difference in my prayer life. In my life as Amish I used a prayer book instead of speaking out of my heart to the savior. There are Biblical teachings that show each of us can have that connection with Jesus. Jeremiah 33:3 says, "Call upon me and I will hear you. I will show you great and mighty things." God has kept His word to me and truly I have no desire to ever go back.

Jesus is my hope, my salvation, my peace in spite
of troubles; my joy in the midst of sorrow, security in the
storm. Indeed, what would I do without
His wonderful presence in my life?
I am secure in Him; now and for eternity.

Chapter Twenty-Two
After Pentecost
- Sister Barbara -

Much of our life is the same as before we came to Abingdon. Jacob and Amos have been a big help in improving the farm house and our four boys in a row, are the produce planting team. Malinda makes sure plenty of fresh, cold Kool-Aid is served up and I enjoy the plants raised in the green house. Each child has a garden and the pleasure of sharing fresh vegetables or selling them at the Farmers' Market. Usually two go at a time. Bennie has become David's right hand man on the farm and at the market. Raising chickens and selling eggs has become the project for Levi, David Jr., and Elam and of course, Malinda helps us all, especially in the house. And Katie's husband, Steven is one of our boys. After helping to get in hay, or plant a field, he loves to take a swim, go on a hike, or play a game of ball. But for the King family, church has become the focal point. No one wants to miss a service or activity.

It is a privilege to be part of the Abingdon United Pentecostal Church. We have a strong, hard working leader, Pastor Robert McCann. Fasting and prayer is the norm and home prayer meetings and fellowship have helped us to truly become a part. The entire church works for fundraising with many days of cooperation at "on site" projects to see the new building completed. This element of working together was also a time of fellowship and enjoyment in the Amish community. But more than a building is the blessings our family has received in the Pentecostal movement.

What a wonderful joy and privilege to have our children in church with the church family, praising our savior who gave His all that we may have this abundant life. In 2004, nine-year-old Levi received the Holy Ghost and was baptized by Pastor McCann. Our friends, Mark and Kristi Dorton, from Christian Life Center were present in that service. Then, February 29, 2004, seven-year-old David, Jr. was baptized and received the gift of the Holy Ghost. He said to have a birthday on leap year would be "cool." It was; it's his spiritual birthday. Next, on a Saturday evening in April of 2004, five-year-old Elam announced that he wanted to be baptized on the morrow. He is a matter-of-fact little guy, but we were amazed that he understood his need. He received the Holy Ghost in that same service. In the Amish movement, the children are usually baptized between the ages of fifteen and twenty years old; thus to have four boys baptized and filled with the Holy Ghost at an early age is an amazing blessing.

When I think of how Jesus sacrificed His life for me, my heart overflows with love and praise. I worship Him with my whole being now and not with merely thinking a prayer. He filled me with His precious Holy Ghost and more than anything else I want to please Him. Jesus loves me so much and He constantly draws my thoughts and heart to Him. He speaks to me as I read His word and when I hear the teaching and preaching of the scripture. God often answers my questions after I pray desiring to know His will. I want to be daily washed, cleansed, and forgiven that I may be able to dwell with Him forever.

The benefits of being a Christian are many in this life. We have many lessons to learn and God is an amazing teacher. He shows up in nature as we do our daily work in the gardens and fields. (And as is usually the case, our children manage to ask some mind stretching questions.) Jesus is my hope, my salvation, my peace in spite of troubles; my joy in the midst of sorrow, security in the storm. Indeed, what would I do without His wonderful presence in my life? I am secure in Him; now and for eternity. Until He comes again, our joy is renewed when we teach a home Bible study and see someone repent, be baptized in Jesus name, and receive the baptism of the Holy Ghost. To God be the glory for all He has done.

Chapter Twenty-Three
From Amish to Apostolic
- Jonathan Miller -

I was born September 5, 1946 in Fairbanks, Iowa. When I was nine-years-old, I broke three bones in my ankle. The cast covered my leg from my knees to my toes. The doctor said I needed the cast and crutches for at least 10-12 weeks. One day, while lying in bed, I felt a hand touch my ankle However, I didn't mention this to my parents. Three days later an X-ray was taken to check the healing process. The doctor said the cast could come off. A miracle had happened...by the unknown touch, yet I never told anyone because I wasn't even sure of it myself.

My family moved to Jamesport, Missouri, in January of 1958. Many times during my teenage years, I woke up through the night and felt that same touch on my shoulder. I didn't feel free to confide in my parents for fear of being rebuked. I can say singing gospel hymns, reading my Bible, and going to church were my most cherished moments growing up.

On January 27, 1966, Emma E. Borkholder and I were united in marriage. We earnestly desired a family, but we endured heartache the next seven years. After our first son's death in November (only 30 hours after birth), we were distraught. Even so, later during a church service, God used a story told by the minister to help us better understand our hurt. The loss of two more daughters and one more son, all stillborn, finally prompted the doctor to suggest that we stop trying to have children. Emma was also diagnosed with diabetes and was told her life could be endangered. Also, in 1973, I lost my precious mother.

Though we suffered emotionally, we believed each trial was another stepping stone leading us closer to God. The Lord was faithful, and gave us eleven foster children and our son, Ryan, who we loved greatly, and got to keep. Emma's health deteriorated with a massive heart attack, leg amputation, vision problems and later she suffered a stroke and paralysis. Since the Amish are taught to be self provisional, we soon became financially and emotionally despondent. But hope was on the way. On our farm in Kentucky, 1990, I was about half-way out to the barn when I thought I heard someone speak. I turned, but no one was there. I found I could not move; I was frozen where I was. "This must be my time," I instantly thought. I spoke to God in my mind. "If this is my time to go Lord, then here I am. I am all yours." Suddenly, a form of a person appeared in front of me. I squinted my eyes from the brightness. A voice spoke. "Be obedient. Preach the Word of God and teach the plan of salvation." As the angel disappeared, I fell on my face and cried out to God. I realized for the first time in my life that there was more I had to do. Amish are taught to use a prayer book, but I had my first experience talking directly to God. I promised God I would obey Him. I knew I was called to do something very special. I was shocked and amazed at this experience with God. I had a speech problem and was very bashful. Why had God visited me in such a fantastic way? My church immediately became my greatest obstacle. They did not deny my experience, but they did not accept it either. The Amish church and family that we loved rejected my calling, we were excommunicated. Praise be to God, only five and a half weeks later I received the gift of the Holy Ghost in a Pentecostal church! Three weeks later, we were all baptized in Jesus name. I finally understood, this is what the angel meant, "Preach the Word of God …teach the plan of salvation." That is exactly what we did until Emma's death in 1998.

Emma had gone home to be with the Lord, but God had a very special person waiting to enter my life. Bridgett is gifted in many ways. She is anointed with a ministry of music. Her songs bring healing and comfort to many as we travel to minister. The Lord has opened many doors for us to minister to other Amish and Mennonite families who desire a deeper relationship with God.

I can truly say that God has restored my life. Where loss and rejection had thrived, I have brothers and sisters who have also left the Amish faith to be baptized in Jesus name, and they have received the gift of the Holy Ghost as recorded in John 3:5 and Acts 2:38. Truly, I am walking in His marvelous light! God bless you and your family as you seek out your own salvation.

Chapter Twenty-Four
Our Testimony
- John Mullet -

My name is John Mullet. We are a family of six which includes my wife, RoseAnna, our four children, Norma Jean, Lena Rose, Homer Dean, and Martha Sue. In 2003, I worked with Aaron Haug who attended an apostolic church. He seemed very cordial and we had discussions about the Bible. Our first real topic was about the Godhead. I believed that God was two persons, God and Jesus Christ. Baptism was the next topic. Aaron showed me where baptism is to be done by immersion in Jesus name. I believed that sprinkling in the name of the Father, Son, and Holy Ghost was sufficient. After a year, I finally told him to let me alone about it. He responded that the Word would always remain the same. Some time later, my wife informed me that she, too, believed in only one God and she also understood water baptism in Jesus name. However, she couldn't bear to think of leaving the Amish to do this. She never wanted to lose her family and friends. She actually fought against her feelings. These were difficult months for her.

In the winter of 2004, there were rumors that we were leaving the Amish. We had been asking questions among our Amish brethren and received different responses. Some got upset and told us to be satisfied with what we had. Although we assured them we were not leaving, we did begin a search for more in God's word. We studied, but still did not consider leaving the Amish. We were satisfied with the standards and had many friends.

We built a new home in 2005; therefore, we didn't talk much about scripture. We knew that people were watching us, but "what is truth?" stayed in the back of our minds.

We had met a couple who attend an apostolic church. In 2006, while discussing the Bible, we began to get a much better understanding of God's word. We enjoyed being with them, and I noticed my wife was comfortable with this, also. One day, after a hard day's work, I was in the shop doing some serious thinking. I finally went into the house to tell Rose that I was going to be baptized in Jesus name. She was upset at first because she wasn't ready to take that step as yet. She was torn between family and friends or obedience to what the Bible teaches. So after going through some difficult days she told me she was willing to be baptized, also. I was overwhelmed with joy when Rose told me she wanted to be baptized with me.

On February 26, 2006, we were baptized in Jesus name. We have not regretted our decision to follow Jesus and His word. Rose had the church elders pray for her and she received an instant healing. It was July 16, 2006 when we received the precious gift of the Holy Ghost and have had many wonderful experiences since then. This has been our first experience living for God where everything is about Jesus instead of the traditions of men.

We will be forever thankful for the wonderful church family that God had given us and for the many prayers that were sent heavenward for us! Praise His name. We wish God's richest blessings upon all who read this and we hope to meet you in heaven someday.

At the Farmers Market in Abingdon.
Elam, Bennie, Audrey holding Michi, and Brother David

About the Author
- Audrey J. Feigl -

Audrey J. Feigl holds a general license with the United Pentecostal Church, International, headquartered in Hazelwood, Missouri. She is mother of four children and grandmother of eight; and more recently a great grandmother. Feigl is primarily a Home Missions preacher at heart. She helped start two new works in Illinois before founding and pastoring the United Pentecostal Church of Highland, Illinois from 1982-1998. She holds an Associate in Applied Science in Law Enforcement and a Bachelor of Science in Occupational Education. She served as feature editor for four years at Belleville Area College, Belleville, Illinois. Besides pastoring in Highland, Feigl had a prison ministry at Menard Penitentiary, Chester, Illinois, for seven years. She was a volunteer chaplain at Anderson Hospital in Maryville, Illinois and radio broadcaster on W.I.N.U. in Highland; first for the radio station and later with a church broadcast. Feigl now resides in Gardners, Pennsylvania with her companion of ten years, Michi, a Chihuahua and also with her sister and brother-in-law, Geraldine and Tom White.

I can truly say that God has restored my life. Where loss and rejection had thrived, I have brothers and sisters who have also left the Amish faith to be baptized in Jesus name, and they have received the gift of the Holy Ghost as recorded in John 3:5 and Acts 2:38.

Further Reading on Anabaptist History

Amish people, Living Plain in A Complex World
Carolyn Meyer
Murray Printing Co. 1976
Forge Valley, MA.

The Amish
Jean Kinney Williams
Franklin Watts 1996
A Division of Grolier Pub.
New York, NY

Dr. Frau, A Women Doctor Among the Amish
Grace H. Kaiser
Good Books, 1986
Intercourse, PA.

Amish Roots, A Treasury of History, Wisdom and Love
John A. Hostetler
The John Hopkins Un. Press, 1989
Baltimore and London

The Gift of Being Simple
Bill Coleman
Chronicle Books 2001
San Francisco, CA

The German peasants War
And Anabaptist Community of Goods
James M. Stayer
McGill-Queens University Press 1991
Canada